Barbara Gibson

Pigs, like humans, can get sunburned. Unlike humans, pigs don't lie in the sun. They seek shade and a cool bath.

Far-out facts

■ BOOKS FOR WORLD EXPLORERS
■ NATIONAL GEOGRAPHIC SOCIETY

Contents

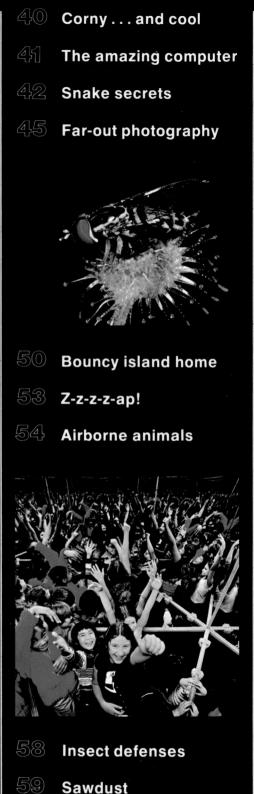

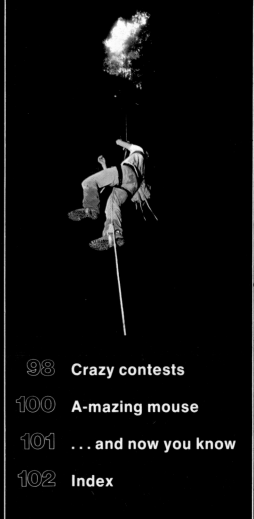

Copyright © 1980 National Geographic Society
Library of Congress
CIP data: p. 104

Odd jobs

Fifty skydivers leap from a huge airplane 16,000 feet (4,876 m)* above Florida. They start forming a star shape. Who photographs them? Other sky-divers! Tom Dunn and Jerry Irwin made the pictures on these pages. Both men have unusual jobs. They make action photographs from the air. Free-falling and parachuting, they follow their subjects from the plane to the ground. An average 12,000-foot (3,658-m) trip lasts 3½ minutes.

These men are not the only people to choose unusual occupations. There are more ways to earn a living than you might think. On the following pages, you'll meet other people with odd jobs.

Moving at 100 miles (161 km) an hour, the skydivers complete their pattern. They are now about a mile (1.6 km) above the ground. Their maneuver set a record as the largest formation ever achieved by jumpers during a free-fall. Seconds after this picture was made, the divers began to separate and open their parachutes.

Shooting as he parachutes, Dunn makes pictures of other divers. A camera is fastened to his helmet. A wire from the camera runs through a sleeve and into one hand. By pressing a button on the end of the wire, he clicks the camera shutter. In the other hand, Dunn holds a steering line attached to his parachute.

Jerry Irwin

Roz Schanzer (both)

Cough counter

Biologist Robert Drummond counts the number of times fish "cough" as they swim in water samples. Coughing is a sign of water pollution.

To breathe, fish have to keep their gills clear. If trash and poisons get into their gills, fish can't breathe easily. They try to force the harmful substances out. The movement of the gills disturbs the water. Instruments record the disturbances as peaks in a line on a chart. Fish may begin coughing and breathing faster if their environment has as little as $\frac{1}{100}$ part of certain harmful chemicals to a million parts of water.

Drummond works for the U. S. Environmental Protection Agency in Duluth, Minnesota. When he spots a sudden increase in fish coughs, he knows something is wrong with the water.

"We count recorded fish coughs by hand," Drummond says. "Now, we're trying to teach a computer to do the counting. Our biggest problem is getting the computer to count only the right peaks in the chart line. Not all peaks are coughs. Some may be yawns or sighs. We have found that fish also cough when they are excited or startled. As a result, we have stopped making unnecessary trips to the room where the fish are kept."

Seed detective

Charles Gunn is a detective. He studies clues and investigates mysteries—using seeds!

Dr. Gunn works for the U. S. Department of Agriculture. He identifies "mystery seeds" by comparing them with other seeds in a huge collection. Cabinets in Dr. Gunn's office are filled with seeds—90,000 kinds—from all over the world. He knows the names of many at a glance.

Archaeologists ask Dr. Gunn to identify seeds from ancient cities. The police call on him to see if seeds in a suspect's clothing match those from the scene of a crime. His detective work has saved lives. He discovered that some black-and-red seeds used in imported necklaces were poisonous! Sales of the necklaces were quickly stopped. He saved a boy's life by identifying deadly seeds the boy had swallowed. This information helped doctors decide on the right treatment.

Cricket keepers

The sound of crickets is sweet music to the Larry Hockin family of Farwell, Michigan. The Hockins raise and sell about ten million crickets each year. Most are used as fish bait. Some go to pet stores and zoos as food for snakes and birds. Kipp Hockin, 13, harvests crickets by shaking them off the frames where they roost. After they're poured into boxes, the crickets are mailed to customers.

Scent sniffer

A nose that knows perfume belongs to Serge Kalougive of the city of Grasse, in France. He works for a company that makes perfume. When a new perfume is being developed, he may sniff several thousand scents. He carefully chooses a few. Then he blends them to make the perfume. The process may take years. Because of their unusual skill, perfume sniffers are called "noses."

Roz Schanzer (above)

James A. Sugar (below)

7

Still life

Three models and one mannequin (say MAN-ih-kin) are on display at a shopping center near Washington, D. C. (left). Merchants sometimes pose mannequins, or store dummies, with live models. They hope the unusual combination will attract the attention of passing shoppers. It often does (below). On jobs like this, models have to remain absolutely still. They can't talk, laugh, twitch, scratch, or move their eyes.

"A few people start telling jokes. They try to make you laugh," says Madeleine Boyer. She's the one in the plaid jacket. "I usually hold a pose for about half an hour," says Miriam De Los Rios, left. "My longest time was an hour. You look at one spot and blank out everything else." Also posing are Amy High, seated, and a nameless companion.

Models clown with their fiberglass co-star (right). They say people sometimes try to find out if they are real by tugging on them.

Sisse Brimberg and Nelson Brown, NGS (all)

9

Birdman of London

Ravensmaster John Wilmington lives at the Tower of London in England (above). His special job is caring for the big, black ravens that also live at the famous tower.

Ravens are relatives of the crow. There have been ravens at the Tower of London for hundreds of years. According to one story, the birds squawked an alarm in 1660 when enemy soldiers tried to capture the tower. Afterward, the story spread that England would fall if the ravens ever left the tower.

To try to keep the birds happy, the government pays for their food, and appoints a ravensmaster to care for them. He clips their wings and feeds them dog biscuits and ground meat. At night, the birds are housed in a protected enclosure.

John Wilmington feeds a snack to a raven (left). He makes sure no harm comes to the birds at the Tower of London. Sometimes ravens peck the ankles of visitors who walk around the grounds.

Warning! Hands off!

A colorful caterpillar creeps along a branch. It looks harmless, and it is only about 2 inches (5 cm) long. But you wouldn't want to touch it. Spines on this caterpillar's skin contain a poisonous substance. It irritates the skin of other creatures. The caterpillar is the larva, or young form, of the io (say EYE-oh) moth. Many kinds of ios live in the Western Hemisphere. Stinging spines help these caterpillars survive. When an io caterpillar turns into a moth, it has a different defense (below).

Markings called eyespots may help the io moth survive. When the moth is at rest, folded wings hide the spots. If threatened by a hungry bird, the moth unfolds its wings. Experts believe the "eyes" may startle and confuse the enemy.

Up in the air

Trained Atlantic bottlenose dolphin leaps into the air. Bottlenose dolphins can jump as high as 24 feet (7 m) above the surface of the water. That's more than three times as high as a human being can jump! Bottlenose dolphins are air-breathing sea mammals. They are powerful swimmers and jumpers. If rewarded with praise and food, they can be taught to do acrobatics.

Fantastic frogs

Sticky fingers and toes give the tree frog a good grip on things. It can even hang on to a vertical pane of glass! Tree frogs are tiny acrobats. The smallest are less than an inch (2 cm) long. They have round pads on their fingers and toes. Glands in the pads ooze a sticky substance that helps the frogs climb and cling.

Yva Momatiuk

Frogs have to look before they leap. While they're airborne, they can't see. At takeoff, muscles pull a frog's big, bulging eyes into their sockets. Lower lids close over the eyes, protecting their delicate surfaces.

D. J. Lyons

Most animal dads don't help raise the young. But some male frogs do all the baby-sitting. The female corroboree (say kuh-ROB-uh-ree) frog lays her eggs in a moss nest. The male (below) guards the eggs until they hatch.

Stanley Breeden

F. Gohier/Nat'l Audubon Soc. Coll./PR

This frog is hiding some tadpoles. Can you guess where? When the eggs of a Darwin's frog are about to hatch, the male opens his mouth and scoops them up. He keeps the tadpoles inside his vocal sac for about three weeks.

13

Pedal-powered plane

Bryan Allen did something no one else had ever done. On June 12, 1979, he crossed the English Channel in an aircraft powered only by human muscles! Allen pedaled a 75-pound (34-kg) flying machine. It looked like a bicycle enclosed in a thin shell. It had a propeller in the back, a small control wing in the front, and one very long, narrow wing overhead. Pedaling turned the propeller and kept the craft in the air.

A team of engineers in California built this flying machine. They named it *Gossamer Albatross*. "Gossamer" refers to something very light and thin. An albatross is a seabird with long wings.

Allen trained for months before attempting the flight. Even then, it wasn't easy. He had to pedal fast, without letup, to cross the Channel from

Flying above the water, the Gossamer Albatross *heads for France. Bryan Allen, a biologist from Bakersfield, California, pedals hard inside the cabin. The craft never climbed more than 30 feet (9 m) above the water.*

Otis Imboden, NGS

Allen trains by pedaling an exercise bicycle. For the flight across the English Channel, he worked out at least two hours a day. Joe Mastropaolo, right, coached him.

England to France, a distance of about 22 miles (35 km).

Along the way, he ran into rough air that slowed him down. The radio transmitter didn't work. The cabin grew hot and steamy. It became hard for him to see where he was going.

He pedaled so long and hard to keep the *Albatross* in the air that he had severe leg cramps. He ran out of drinking water. Several times, the plane was only a few inches above the Channel. But he kept telling himself: "Can't give up. Got to keep going." And at last — after nearly three hours — he made it to land!

Wearing a bicycle helmet, a plastic foam life belt, shorts, and biking shoes, Allen takes the Albatross *up for a ten-minute test. Such flights helped the builders make sure the craft was in top working order for its real test, the flight across the Channel.*

Allen signs autographs for French children after his successful landing. You can read more about the history-making journey of the Gossamer Albatross *in the November 1979 issue of* NATIONAL GEOGRAPHIC.

James A. Sugar (both)

Space walker

Far-out equipment enables astronauts to walk in space. This sealed suit was developed for the Gemini 4 mission in 1965. It protected the body from extremes of temperature and the lack of air pressure. A cord linked the space walker to his capsule. Gold tape wrapped around the cord protected it from harmful heat rays. To move, the astronaut fired compressed air from a special gun.

James A. McDivitt/NASA

17

Fancy fish

You probably won't see goldfish like these in your neighborhood. They are fancy goldfish, and all are rare relatives of the fish you may have in a bowl at home.

People in the Orient began breeding such fish about a thousand years ago. Now they ship them all over the world.

Some owners take their fancy fish to shows, where they are judged on form and coloring, somewhat as cats and dogs are.

Fancy goldfish are expensive, and many need special care. A very unusual one may sell for more than $1,000.

Tom Myers

Bubble vision. The fish known as a bubble eye (left) has large, soft sacs below its eyes. The sacs are filled with liquid.

Fancy fish called a lionhead wears a face mask (below). The lumpy mask keeps growing as long as the fish lives. Breeders and owners give the fish high-protein food to help the mask grow.

Fish with eyebrows? Not really. The pompon just looks as if it has eyebrows. The "brows" are really bunches of soft flesh. They grow from the fish's nostrils, which are near the eyes.

Paul A. Zahl, NGS (bottom, both)

Long fins, a humped back, and an extra-long tail identify the fish called a Japanese Ryukin (say rye-YOU-kin). The top fin stands up like a sail in a breeze.

These goldfish aren't gold colored (below). They are Moors, prized for their black coloring. As Moors grow older, they may become lighter in color. Usually they turn reddish or gold.

Celestials have large upturned eyes. The eyes seem to gaze toward heaven. According to one story, monks in Korea first developed this breed of fish for a temple pond.

PENCILS

The pencil is an amazing tool. An average seven-inch (18-cm) pencil could draw a line 35 miles (56 km) long if it were used right to the end without wasting any material in sharpening. Americans buy more than <u>two billion</u> pencils each year. With normal use, that many pencils could draw a line 15 billion miles (24 billion km) long. That's twice the round-trip distance to the planet Pluto!

The pencil got its start as a small disk of lead. Ancient Greeks and Romans used it to draw guidelines for writing. The writing itself was done with a tiny brush called a *pencillus*. Many centuries later, people began writing with a thin piece of lead in a wooden holder. The "lead" in modern pencils isn't lead at all. It's graphite. This soft black substance was accidentally uncovered in England in 1564. A big tree fell down exposing graphite under the ground. For pencil makers and people who just like to doodle, it was a happy discovery.

They say it's from earth!

Jan Watkins (all)

"Sometimes I wonder if it's worth lighting a candle!"

People have used fire for thousands of years, but they've been able to make it easily only since 1816. That's when the match was invented. Before that, people started fires by rubbing sticks together or by striking flint on metal to make sparks.

Early match heads had to be scratched very hard. They produced a shower of sparks and smoke that smelled like rotten eggs. They were called Lucifers because they made some people think of the devil.

Americans now use about 550 billion matches a year. Machines make them. A machine can make a million wooden matches in an hour.

Wonder-full world

How hot, cold, rainy, or dry does the earth get? Where are its highest and lowest spots? What is the largest island? The deepest part of the ocean? Did you know the date line splits an island nation in two? Read more startling facts about our earth on the following pages.

You may think the widest series of waterfalls in the world is found at Niagara. Not so. Iguazú (say ee-gwah-soo) Falls in South America is twice as wide. Water there plunges over a series of rocky rims that stretch for $2^{1}/_{2}$ miles (4 km). They form a long, narrow "J" shape. Like Niagara, which lies on the border between the United States and Canada, Iguazú Falls straddles two countries. The long part of the "J" is in Argentina. The short end is in Brazil.

Loren McIntyre

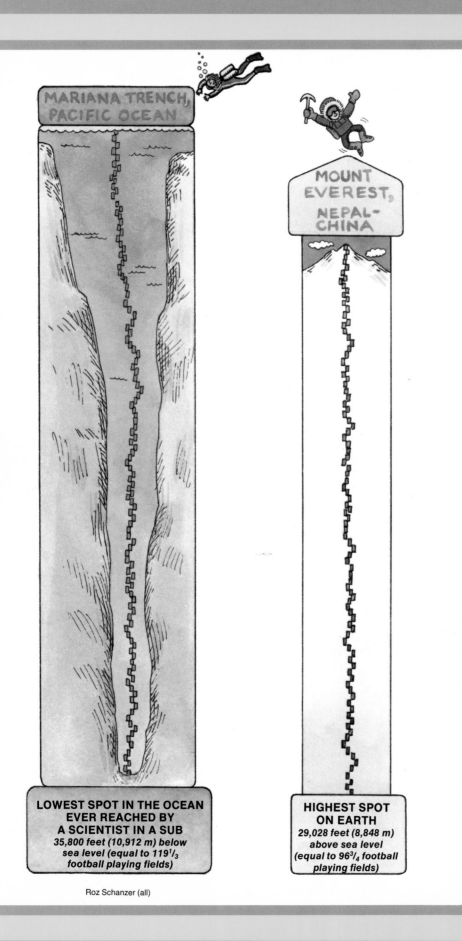

MARIANA TRENCH, PACIFIC OCEAN

LOWEST SPOT IN THE OCEAN EVER REACHED BY A SCIENTIST IN A SUB
35,800 feet (10,912 m) below sea level (equal to 119$\frac{1}{3}$ football playing fields)

MOUNT EVEREST, NEPAL-CHINA

HIGHEST SPOT ON EARTH
29,028 feet (8,848 m) above sea level (equal to 96$\frac{3}{4}$ football playing fields)

Roz Schanzer (all)

DEAD SEA, ISRAEL-JORDAN

LOWEST SPOT ON EARTH
1,302 feet (397 m) below sea level (equal to 4$\frac{1}{3}$ football playing fields)

Super mine

You're looking at the largest hole ever dug by humans (right). It's the Bingham open-pit copper mine near Salt Lake City, Utah. The mine, begun in 1906, is now almost half a mile (805 m) deep. It is 2$\frac{1}{2}$ miles (4 km) wide at the top. Railroad tracks wind around it and carry cars that haul out the copper ore. The mine has produced more copper than any other mine in history.

James L. Amos, NGS (right)

What day is this?

Do you ever forget what day it is? Most people do once in a while. But you'd have an even harder time keeping things straight if you lived in Kiribati (say kee-ree-BAHS).

This island nation in the Pacific takes life two days at a time. The date line runs between some of the islands. When it is Sunday on one side of the date line, it is Monday on the other. Some people are relaxing while others are at work or in school.

The 33 islands of Kiribati became an independent nation in 1979. Before that, they belonged to the British.

Kiribatians fish and harvest coconuts. They ship the dried coconut meat, called copra (say COPE-ruh), all over the world. About a third of the people live on Tarawa (say tuh-RAH-wuh), where the capital is located.

Jay Groff

MT. WAIALEALE, HAWAII

RAINIEST SPOT ON EARTH
(say wy-ahl-ee-AHL-ee)
Annual average, 460 inches (11,684 mm)

Roz Schanzer

Record setters

No rainfall has ever been recorded in parts of this desert. Yet things grow! Fog from the Pacific Ocean and snowmelt from nearby mountains provide moisture.

ATACAMA DESERT, CHILE

WATER!

(say at-uh-KAHM-uh)
DRIEST SPOT ON EARTH
Rainfall is barely measurable.

Roz Schanzer (all)

AL ʿAZĪZĪYAH, LIBYA

(say al-ah-zee-ZEE-yah)
HOTTEST SPOT ON EARTH
136°F (58°C) recorded in 1922

Does it ever get as hot as 100°F (38°C) where you live? Then imagine living in this desert town in northern Africa. Yet in spite of the heat, trees and grains grow nearby. People also manage to raise farm animals.

Fierce winds batter Vostok, a Soviet scientific station. It stands on an ice plateau nearly 2¹/₂ miles (4 km) high.

VOSTOK, ANTARCTICA

COLDEST SPOT ON EARTH
-127°F (-88°C) recorded in 1960

What's under the ice?

Greenland is the world's largest island. But it's not all above sea level. If you could lift the ice cap and look beneath it, you would see a ring of mountains and a lot of water. The ice cap is two miles (3 km) thick in places and very heavy. The weight of the ice has pushed down the center of Greenland until a third of the land lies more than 1,000 feet (305 m) below the surface of the sea.

Jaime Quintero

Makeup

Imagine your face covered with pig grease, stripes, or dots. If you lived in some parts of the world, that's what you might wear on special occasions. People in nearly every land use makeup. But they don't use the same kinds. Makeup may show what tribe or religious group the wearer belongs to. It may mark a person as important or special in some way. It may simply be worn for beauty. Not everyone, of course, agrees on what looks beautiful. The pictures on these pages show how some people decorate their faces.

Young Japanese girl of Kyoto wears chalk-white makeup, similar to the makeup worn in traditional Japanese plays. The girl is a maiko (say MY-ee-ko), an apprentice geisha (say GAY-shuh). Apprentices spend several years learning to sing, dance, and play a musical instrument. Then they entertain at parties and tea houses. As more Japanese adopt western customs, very few classical geisha remain.

Thomas Höpker, Woodfin Camp & Assoc.

Jack Fields

In Papua New Guinea, an island nation near Australia, some women wear makeup with a pattern of dots. First, they rub on pig grease. Then, they add powdered red paint. Finally, they paint on bright markings and colored dots. The makeup is intended to make them look attractive.

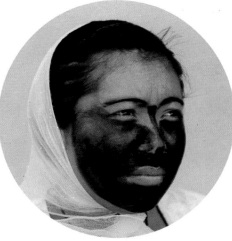

Loren McIntyre

Dark paint covers most of the face of a Guajiro (say gwa-HE-ro) Indian woman in the country of Colombia, in South America. Such paint once had special meaning. It showed whether a woman was married or single. Now Indians wear it as decoration and to protect their skin from wind and sun.

Red dot on the forehead of a boy in India shows he is a Hindu. The dot, called a tika (say TEE-kuh), symbolizes good fortune. Boys wear tikas on special occasions, along with decorative markings. They put on the symbols after a bath. Hindus believe bathing cleanses both body and spirit.

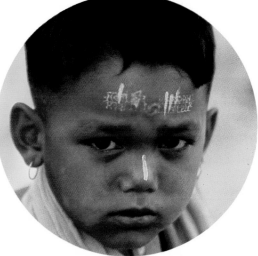

Jehangir Gazdar, Woodfin Camp & Assoc.

John J. Putman, NGS

Orange makeup symbolizes strength in an African tribesman (left). He is a candidate for the post of temporary chief of the village. During an election ceremony, the grand chief of the region considers the abilities of the chosen leader. Flutes and drums play. When the grand chief gives final approval, a messenger will rush to the new chief and mark his forehead with a line of white powder.

Jerry Burn

Compared to the other people on these pages, a New York City model looks as if she has no makeup on. But she does. She is wearing eye makeup, rouge, and lipstick. The result: a "natural" look popular in many Western countries.

How would you like to look today?

Molly Atkinson, 10, wanted to look like a big cat. When she visited Busch Gardens, in Tampa, Florida, she had her chance. Artist Dennis Phillips gave Molly a cat face in seven minutes. Many artists paint faces at fairs and parks. They use harmless stage makeup that washes off. By the time Molly went home to Frederick, Maryland, she looked like herself again.

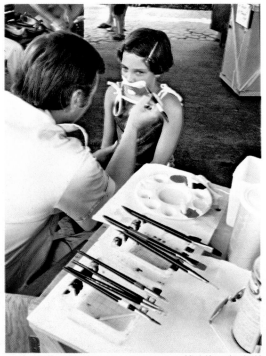

Mitch Kezar (top both)

Clowning around with makeup

A clown without makeup is like a zig without a zag. Here, a clown gets ready for a performance with the Clyde Beatty-Cole Bros. Circus. First, he puts on thick white stage makeup (left). Next, he will add blue lips and eyebrows, and other markings (right). Bold lines and bright colors help people in the audience see the clown's painted expression during the show. The audience can tell from the makeup whether the clown is happy or sad.

A clown puts on makeup in the same way for every performance. The makeup is called a "working face." Each person who becomes a clown tries to design an original working face. The face then becomes that clown's personal trademark.

Odd ideas that worked

Many of the world's great inventions were happy accidents. Sometimes inventors stumbled onto an idea. Sometimes they made a mistake that worked out well. And sometimes a gadget made for one job turned out to have other uses, often more uses than the inventor could have imagined.

Barbara Gibson (both)

In the chips

In 1853, a restaurant customer criticized the fried potatoes of chef George Crum. "Too thick," said the customer. "Too soggy, and not salty enough." Crum sliced potatoes paper thin. He fried the slices to a crisp, and he salted them heavily. The diner liked the crunchy potato chips. So did other people. Now, Americans turn $3\frac{1}{2}$ billion pounds ($1\frac{1}{2}$ billion kg) of potatoes into chips each year.

Flavor and fizz

When early settlers came to America, they brought recipes for tasty drinks with them. They made the drinks from herbs and weeds. Often they added yeast. This produced bubbles, which made the drinks fizz. The settlers found that American Indians had good-tasting drinks of their own. They made them out of roots and barks, such as licorice and birch. As the settlers and Indians traded ideas, they came up with a new drink. It combined American flavoring and European fizz. The new drink? Root beer.

Punch-a-picture

In the 1880s, engineer Herman Hollerith was searching for a fast way to record census information. He found it on a train. He saw a conductor punching holes in tickets. The position of each hole told something about the ticket holder, such as hair or eye color. If the "passenger" turned out to be a train robber, this record would help the police. Hollerith designed punched cards for an electric computing machine. Each hole gave the answer to a question. The machine counted the holes, and the ancestor of the computer was born. Read more about computers on page 41.

Barbara Gibson

Instant wheels

Try these gadgets for speed and a good time. Push a button.

Wheels pop out of the sole of your shoe. Hit the button again. The wheels disappear. The shoe-skates were designed in 1961 for Swiss factory workers.

The inventor hoped the skates would make the workers faster at their jobs. Now Pop Wheels are sold in many places. Most people use them just for fun.

Jan Watkins

Tired of strolling?   *Pop the wheels . . .*   *and you'll get rolling!*

Glue, not dew, glistens on a plant called a sundew. It is one of many meat-eating plants. The sparkle and

Meat-eating plants

Everyone has seen an animal eating a plant. Few people have seen the opposite: a plant eating an animal. But some plants do just that.

Meat-eating plants are found in many parts of the world. There are about 450 kinds. Soil in the marshy areas where the plants grow does not provide enough nourishment for them. They trap insects and other small creatures for food.

Most of these plants give off a sweet-smelling liquid, or nectar, that attracts animals. The plants trap the animals in various ways. Some plants have leaves that snap shut. Others are like sticky flypaper. Still others are cup-shaped. The cups hold poisonous liquid or water that drowns the victims. Meat-eating plants can't hurt humans. Most trap only insects.

Trapped by sticky liquid, a fly tries to escape. The harder it struggles, the more glue it touches. Slowly, the tentacles bend toward the fly and close in. Digestive juices in the plant will absorb the meal within a few hours.

John Shaw, Bruce Coleman Inc.

scent of the liquid droplets attract insects.

Dwight R. Kuhn

Plants called bladderworts bloom among water lilies in a swamp. Beneath the surface of the water, bladderwort

A common wild plant, the bladderwort lives in ponds. It has no roots, but its stems are covered with thousands of hollow pods. Each pod is about as big as a grape seed, and each has fine hairs and a trapdoor. When a tiny creature touches the hairs, the trapdoor springs open. The pod sucks in the creature, and the door closes. It all happens faster than you can blink.

pods trap food.

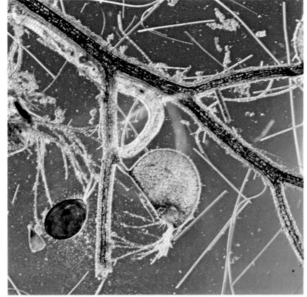

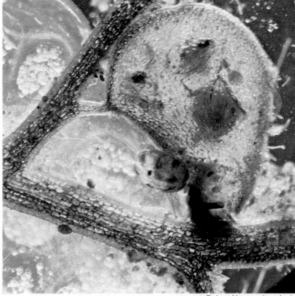

Robert Noonan (top, both)

Tiny animal called an ostracod (say OS-truh-kod), at lower left, feeds near a bladderwort pod. The pod grows in the shape of a half circle. It trails long hairs.

Another ostracod comes dangerously close to the mouth of a pod (above). If the ostracod touches trigger hairs, it will join other creatures inside the thin pod walls.

Pitcher plants are brightly colored. Their cups are filled with fragrant liquid. This combination can be deadly to insects. A dip in the pool is a one-way trip. Wingless creatures can't climb out. Wet wings keep insects like the leafhopper (below) from flying out. The liquid dissolves and digests the trapped prey.

John Shaw, Bruce Coleman Inc.

One more step and this ant will be in deep trouble. The lip of the pitcher plant is slippery. Insects that crawl too close to the edge lose their grip. Down they go, into the liquid. Loose, dusty wax covers the inside walls of the pitcher. If insects try to scramble out, their feet become coated with wax, and they slide back into the pool.

Paul A. Zahl, NGS

Every leaf of a Venus's-flytrap (above) is a set of jaws.

Sweet liquid lures insects inside.

Ready . . . Venus's-flytrap remains open while a fly, seeking nectar, lands on the rim of its jaws.

Set . . . When the fly brushes against sensitive trigger hairs deep inside the leaf, the trap will spring shut.

Snap! The jaws close with the fly inside. The trap now becomes a stomach. Juices will digest the meal.

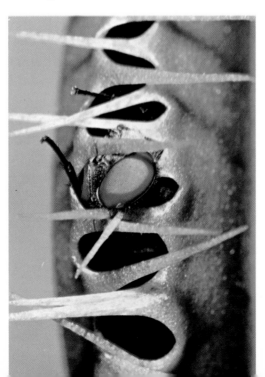

Narrow escape! A grasshopper sits on top of a trap that has sprung. By pushing hard against the sides of a closing trap, a large insect like a grasshopper can sometimes struggle its way to freedom.

Corny... and cool

What a corny building! When people say that about the structure at right, they aren't being insulting. They are giving a good description of the Corn Palace.

The first Corn Palace in Mitchell, South Dakota, was built for a harvest festival held in 1892. Townspeople nailed split ears of corn and bundles of grasses to the walls, forming patterns. As the festival grew over the years, larger palaces were built.

Every summer, artists draw new pictures for the walls. Workmen spend weeks filling in the designs with corn and grasses in natural colors.

Visitors use the Corn Palace for meetings all year. Birds like the canyon wren (far right) use it, too. Some people call the palace the world's biggest bird feeder.

Dana Scott Westering

Using only hand tools, such as a pick, a shovel, and a wheelbarrow, a man named Baldasare Forestiere dug a huge underground home. He carved it out of clay near Fresno, California.

Forestiere began digging in about 1906 to escape the summer heat. First he scooped out a kitchen and a bedroom. Then he just kept going. Eventually he dug about 65 rooms and a maze of tunnels. The floor plan (below, left) shows their pattern. Most rooms have openings in the roof to let in light and air.

Forestiere kept working on his home until he died in 1946. He planted shrubs and tropical trees underground. He even added a fish pond and a fireplace for chilly nights.

Today, this unusual home is open to visitors.

Jan Wampler

Dana Scott Westering

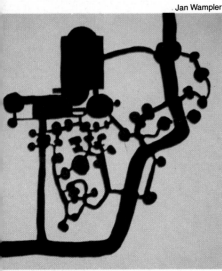

The amazing computer

Circuits on tiny chips start out as designs on huge pieces of film (below). A beam of light guided by a computer draws the design. Then cameras shrink it, and it is printed on a chip.

Would you like to play a tune without a musical instrument? Play chess or word games without a partner? Play team sports inside the house on a rainy day?

No problem. Just call on a computer. It can do amazing things. It is hard to imagine a world without computers.

The first electrical computing device was invented nearly a century ago. It used punched cards to add up figures for the United States Census of 1890. (You can read about it on page 33.) The first computer with a "memory" didn't come along until 1946. It was a huge machine that filled a room the size of a gym. The work it did in four hours would have taken a person 1,500 years!

That's a lot of work. But today's computers can do more, with less bulk. An electronic chip small enough to go through the eye of a darning needle can store up to 64,000 bits of information. Computer speeds are no longer measured in seconds. They are measured in billionths of a second, or nanoseconds.

The chips have made it possible to reduce giant computers to the size of a typewriter. Now, researchers are thinking even smaller. They hope to reduce them to the size of this book.

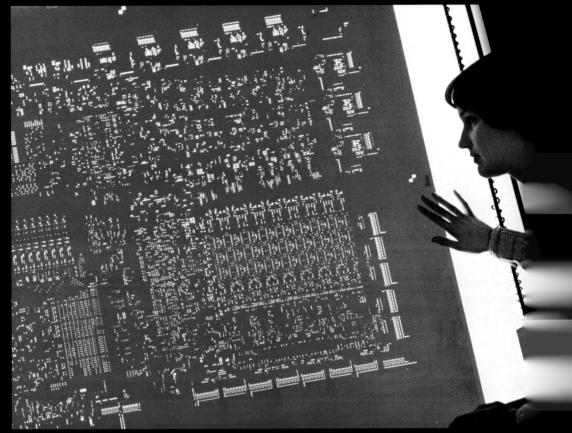

Dan McCoy/Rainbow   Jack Caspary/Woodfin Camp & Assoc.   Bruce Dale, NGS

Plastic strip collects a memory chip on each printed circuit design. Cut apart, they'll be used in computers.

Silicon chip shown on a fingertip (above) can remember 1,000 eight-letter words. Printed on the chip are nearly invisible wires. They connect thousands of microscopic on-off switches. Chips like this are used in computer games.

Snake secrets

When compared with other creatures, snakes seem to lack advantages. Snakes can't walk, run, or fly. They don't have keen hearing. They don't have hands. But snakes have special advantages that help them survive. They have long, thin, flexible bodies. This lets them curl up in small hiding places, slither through narrow openings, and wrap themselves around prey. Some snakes have venom, or poison, that helps them paralyze prey and defend themselves. Others have chemicals in their bodies that produce unpleasant smells. Most snakes have coloring that helps hide them. A few also have ways of tricking their enemies.

San Bernardino ringneck snake ▶

San Bernardino ringneck snake displays the bright underside of its tail when threatened. An enemy attacking the tail will miss the head. The snake may be wounded, but it probably will survive.

San Bernardino ringneck snake

John R. MacGregor

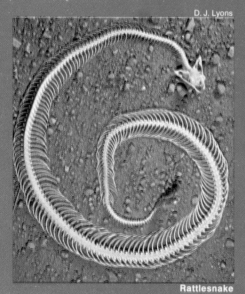

D. J. Lyons

Rattlesnake

▲ *Human adults have 26 bones in their spines. Wriggly snakes have many more. A rattlesnake may have as many as 200. Each pair of ribs is attached to a vertebra in the spinal column. Muscles attached to the ribs enable the snake to slither.*

Rough green snake

◄ *Look at these leaves. The middle "leaf" is a rough green snake. Its coloring blends with the leaves and helps it hide. This is called camouflage (say KAM-uh-flazh). Do you know about any other animals that have camouflage?*

If looks could kill, the Eastern ► hognose snake would zap its enemies on the spot. Flattening its head and flicking its tongue, the harmless hognose looks somewhat like a poisonous snake about to strike. The hognose also has other tricks.

Eastern hognose snake

Eastern hognose snake

▲ *If threatening actions don't scare an enemy, perhaps threatening noises will. The hognose snake fills its lungs with air and expels the air in a loud hiss. It opens its mouth and strikes, but it has no venom.*

▲ *The enemy wasn't frightened by the threat display or the noise. So the hognose snake flops over on its back and plays dead. If nothing happens, it will slowly turn and look around. If the enemy is still lurking nearby, the hognose may flop down and play dead once more.*

◄ *You can't breathe while you swallow, but a snake can. A snake swallows food whole. As it eats, a snake pushes the open end of its windpipe forward to the edge of its mouth. Even a big mouthful of food doesn't block the passage of air.*

Northern pine snake

Far-out photography

The photograph on the left shows a huge crowd of people. Or does it? Look carefully at the "crowd." You'll find there's less to this scene than meets the eye. In fact, there are only eight people in the photograph. The rest of the "people" are reflections.

Twelve mirrors surround the small group like walls. The mirrors bounce the reflections back and forth. This multiplies them many times. The eye is fooled — at least for a moment.

The eye is easily fooled when rays of light are bent or reflected. Photographers may use special lenses or camera techniques to distort, or change, the light and create illusions on film.

Photographers also capture things that the human eye doesn't normally see. Some things happen so fast the eye can't record them. A camera can. Some things change or move slowly, so slowly the eye can't trace the motion. A camera can. Some things are so small the eye can't observe them. But a camera attached to a microscope can.

On the following pages, you'll see examples of some kinds of far-out photography.

Eight's a crowd at a museum exhibit called the hall of mirrors. It's part of The Exploratorium, a science museum in San Francisco, California. The Exploratorium encourages young visitors to learn by doing. Its hall of mirrors has 12 sides. Each is a mirror on legs. The mirrors touch, forming a 12-sided enclosure. Youngsters duck under the panels to enter the enclosure. When they stand up and look around, they get a surprise! They seem to be surrounded by a great many familiar faces.

Dan McCoy/Rainbow

45

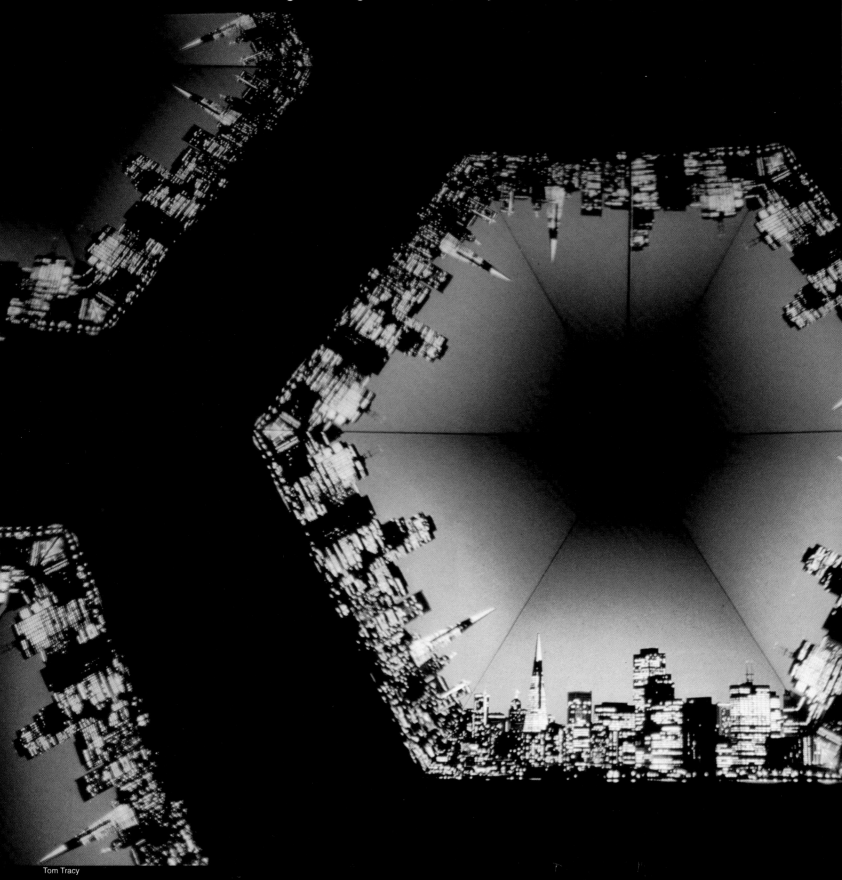

sky at sunset. Mirror seams cut the sky into wedges.

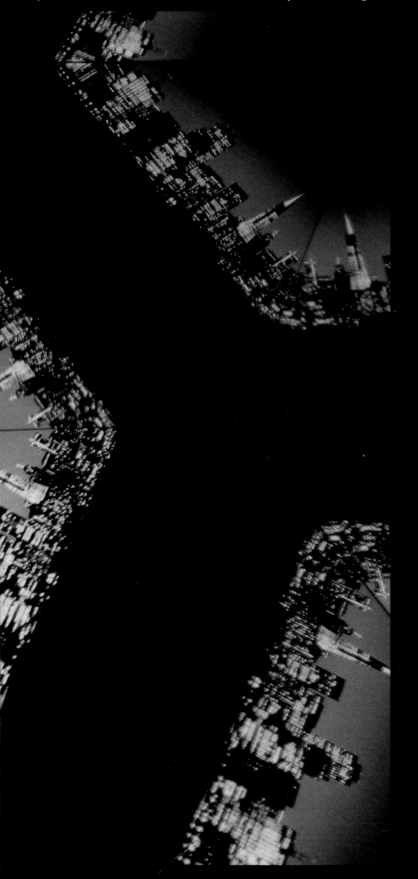

...with mirrors,

The buildings at left seem to be on a merry-go-round. But they aren't moving, and neither is the photographer. He did this trick with mirrors set up to form a giant kaleidoscope (say kuh-LIE-duh-skope). You may have seen a tube-shaped toy kaleidoscope. When you look through an opening in one end, you see a brightly colored pattern. As you turn the other end, bits of plastic tumble about. Mirrors behind them reflect and multiply them, forming designs. The photographer who made this picture arranged three large mirrors in the shape of a pup tent. Instead of plastic pieces, he used a picture of the San Francisco skyline, shot from the Bay Bridge. He projected the picture through a cloudy plastic screen, onto the mirrors. Then he photographed what the mirrors reflected.

John E. Fletcher, NGS

a microscope,

You've seen the substance above many times, but perhaps never like this. It is table salt! A microscope magnified the crystals 50 times. This picture was made using special light filters and a colored background. It shows the shape of the crystals clearly. Each one is a tiny cube.

. . . rippled glass,

You probably don't recognize the young athlete on the right. She is Nadia Comaneci, the famous Romanian gymnast. She is performing on the balance beam. Nadia and the things around her seem to be melting. How did the photographer do it? She put a color slide under a sheet of rippled glass. Then she photographed it through the glass. The ripples bent the rays of light. This produced the kind of image you see when you look at a fish through rippling water.

moving lights,

Lights on an amusement-park ride make a pattern that looks like a giant Slinky toy (below). Passengers on the ride sit in small "spaceships" that hang from a large wheel. As the wheel spins, it slowly rises and tilts. To make this picture, the photographer left the shutter of a camera open for nearly three minutes. Headlights on the "spaceships" trace the action on film. Taillights show as streaks of red.

Tom Tracy

J. Di Maggio/J. Kalish from Peter Arnold, Inc. ▶

... slow motion,

It took a whole year and 48 clicks of the camera shutter to make the photograph at right! The photograph shows the sun tracing a figure eight pattern in the sky. This pattern is called the analemma (say an-uh-LEM-uh). It shows the relationship of the sun to the orbiting, tilted earth during one year. Astronomers, scientists who study the heavens, have drawn pictures of the analemma for centuries. But it was not until 1978 that anyone made a complete record of it on film. The photographer put a camera with a dark lens filter in a window. He hooked it up to a timer. Nearly every week, the camera snapped a picture at 8:30 a.m. Three times during the year, the photographer opened the shutter at dawn and left it open until 8:30. The sun made three streaks of light. They marked the longest day of the year, the shortest day, and August 30, one of two days that year when the loops crossed.

Dennis DiCicco/Sky & Telescope

J. Kim Vandiver & Harold Edgerton

and fast action

Quicker than a wink, a bullet zips above a candle. Shock waves fan out behind it in a V shape. The waves are invisible to the unaided eye. A special kind of photography captures them. The secret lies in mirrors, light, and timing. The photographer worked in a darkened room. First, he set up two curved mirrors facing each other. Next, he set up a powerful light so that when it flashed, its beam would pass through a tiny hole in a screen. Then he opened the camera shutter and fired a handgun. This set off the flash. One blindingly bright beam bounced from mirror to mirror for one third of a millionth of a second. In that split second, the bullet and its shock waves sped between the mirrors, disturbing some light rays. The camera caught these rays. The picture at right was the result.

Bouncy island home

How would you like to live on an island built of reeds? Some Indians in South America do. Their home is a pile of reeds about 7 feet (2 m) high (below). The top of the pile forms an island in Lake Titicaca (say tih-tih-KAHK-uh). This lake is one of the highest in the world. It is $2\frac{1}{2}$ miles (4 km) above sea level, on the border between Bolivia and Peru.

Uru (say OOH-roo) Indians live on the reed island. When they walk, the "ground" under their feet feels springy. If it stops feeling springy and starts feeling squishy, that's a warning. Some of the reeds have rotted. It's time to make repairs. Reeds grow nearby in the shallow parts of the lake. Every month or two, the Urus cut big bundles and use them to patch holes in their island.

No one knows when the Urus first built reed islands in the lake. Some were there when Spaniards invaded the area about 400 years ago.

Running on reeds, Uru Indian children practice soccer (right). All of the buildings on the island, except the one-room schoolhouse, are made from reeds. The schoolhouse is made from sheets of metal. This building was given to islanders by a church group. Tied to the island, it floats on metal barrels.

Reedy village (below) has no gardens, trees, streets, cars, or buses. It does have about 20 reed houses and a small fleet of reed fishing boats. The Urus eat mostly fish, small birds, and the tender stems of reeds.

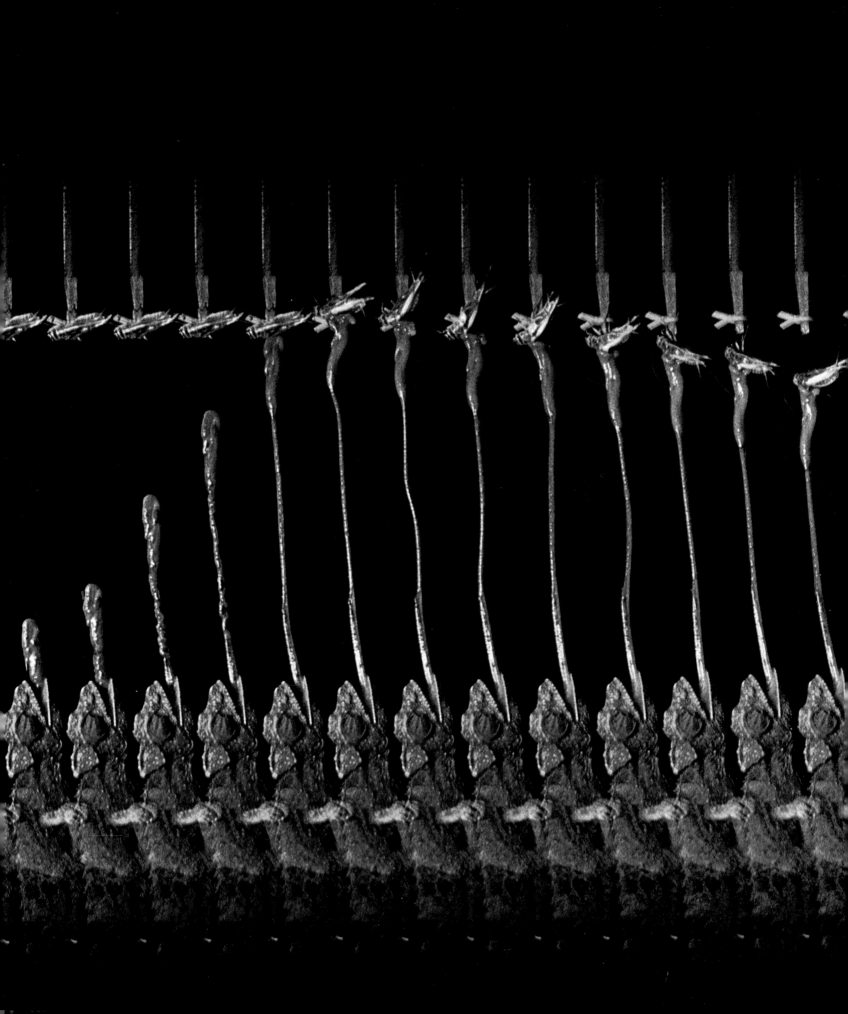

Z-z-z-z-ap!

With perfect aim, a small lizard shoots its tongue toward a cricket. The end of the tongue is shaped like a suction cup. The cup contains a gluey substance that sticks to the cricket. Then the lizard quickly pulls back its tongue — with a meal attached.

This lizard is a chameleon (say kuh-MEEL-yun). It can stretch its tongue until the tongue is longer than its body! The chameleon waits quietly for insects to come within range. Then it zaps them!

The tongue moves so fast the human eye can't follow it. A photographer used special lights and equipment to record this action on film. The chameleon captured its meal within one-tenth of a second!

Lindesay Harkness/Research Fellow, Harvard University

Airborne animals

When you think of birds, you probably think of feathered creatures that fly. All birds do have feathers, and almost all birds fly. But not all of them are alike. In fact, they are amazingly different.

Birds live nearly everywhere in the world. Some nest in trees and bushes, or on buildings and other structures. Some nest on or under the ground. Others spend nearly all their lives at sea. A few, like penguins and ostriches, can't fly.

Nobody knows how many birds there are in the world. Scientists who study these airborne animals say there may be as many as 100 billion. Read about some of them on these and the following pages.

Mitch Kezar
Karl H. Maslowski/Nat'l Audubon Soc. Coll./PR

Great horned owl can turn its head almost all the way around, as this double exposure shows (above). An owl can do this because it has 14 neck bones—twice as many as humans have. An owl cannot move its eyes. Instead, it moves its whole head.

Hard-headed bird, a pileated (say PIE-lee-ate-id) wood-pecker (right) has a thick skull. It helps protect the brain while the woodpecker hammers at trees. The pileated woodpecker chips away wood to uncover insects that bore into trees. It also pecks out holes for nests.

Hovering near a flower, a hummingbird sips sweet liquid called nectar (right). By beating its wings very fast, the hummingbird can stay in one spot in the air. It also can take off straight upward or fly sideways. It can even fly backward—and it is the only bird that can do this! A hummingbird's wings beat as fast as 100 times a second. To the human eye, they appear as a blur. The humming sound of the wings led to the bird's name. Some hummingbirds are less than an inch long.

Bob & Clara Calhoun, Bruce Coleman Inc.

White pelican parents don't serve dinner until their chicks ask for it. Below: A hungry young bird approaches its parent. Squawking loudly, the chick will tap the older bird's bill until the adult opens its mouth. The baby then sticks its head deep inside (left). Up comes partially digested fish for the chick's dinner. When pelicans leave the nest after 10 or 11 weeks, they weigh more than their parents. The young birds live on extra fat while they learn to catch fish.

Harry Engels, Bruce Coleman Inc. (center, right)

Carl-Johan Junge/Emil Lutker (top & bottom)

1

2

Curb service, please! Most birds that eat fish spend a lot of time flying over the water, searching for food. Not the kingfisher! It perches on a branch above the water. Then it waits for dinner to swim past. When it spots a fish it wants to eat, the kingfisher dives into the water ①.

Eyes closed, it grabs the fish in its bill ②. *Then it flaps its way back to the surface* ③. *The bird quickly returns to its perch and kills the fish by smacking its head against the branch. Then the kingfisher swallows its dinner headfirst in a single gulp.*

3

James H. Carmichael, Bruce Coleman Inc.

Dr. E. R. Degginger, Bruce Coleman Inc.

◄ *Meal on the move. A black skimmer scoops up food by dragging the bottom part of its bill in the water. As it skims through the water, the bill gradually wears away. To make up for the wear, the bottom part grows faster.*

Taking off, this blue jay reveals many ► *kinds of feathers. Long, curved feathers, called primaries, spread from the wing tips. Each feather twists as the jay's wings flap, pushing the bird forward. White-tipped wing feathers, called secondaries, help lift the bird in flight. Tail feathers aid in steering and in braking for a landing. Breast feathers, called contours, give the bird's body a smooth surface. Fluffy feathers, or down, are close to the skin. They help insulate the bird.*

Food for color. Flamingos (above) are pink because of substances in their food called carotenoids (say ka-ROT-uhn-oyds). If flamingos do not eat the right kinds of water plants and sea creatures, they may lose their color.

Russ Hansen

Insect defenses

Insects defend themselves in surprising ways. Some use chemical warfare. Their bodies may produce substances that smell or taste bad. The insects may shower their enemies with hot liquid. Often such insects have bright coloring. That warns other creatures to stay away.

If attacked, this African grasshopper squirts a big batch of bubbles (top right). The bubbles smell bad and taste bitter. Although some people and many animals eat grasshoppers, most learn to avoid this one.

E. S. Ross (above & below)

When the darkling beetle does a headstand (right), watch out! It is about to squirt a bad-smelling liquid as a defense. This large black beetle lives in very dry parts of North America.

Bombardier beetles scald their enemies. If threatened, they spray a fluid as hot as boiling water, 212°F (100°C)! This defense discourages small attackers such as ants, and most large ones, such as frogs. Bombardier beetles are found in most parts of the world.

Chip Clark/Smithsonian Institution (bottom)

Sawdust

Every year, lumber mills in the United States pile up 15 million tons (14 million t) of sawdust. What can be done with all that sawdust? A lot of things. Read on.

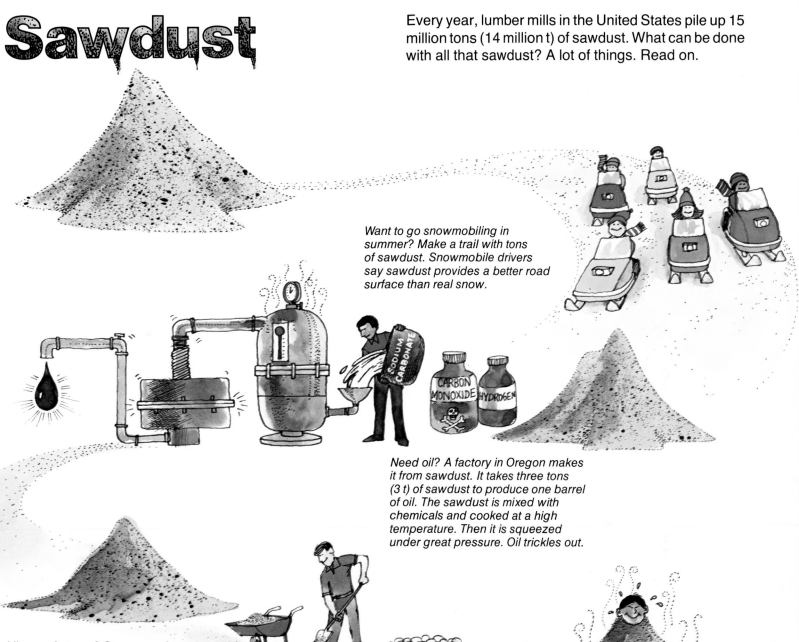

Want to go snowmobiling in summer? Make a trail with tons of sawdust. Snowmobile drivers say sawdust provides a better road surface than real snow.

Need oil? A factory in Oregon makes it from sawdust. It takes three tons (3 t) of sawdust to produce one barrel of oil. The sawdust is mixed with chemicals and cooked at a high temperature. Then it is squeezed under great pressure. Oil trickles out.

Like mushrooms? Some people plant them in decaying sawdust. They put the sawdust in a dark place and add plant food to provide extra nourishment.

Feeling tired? Achy? Sweat out your symptoms in sawdust. That's what some people in Japan do. They pay a doctor to bury them up to their necks in sawdust that contains certain heat-producing chemicals. The patients sweat heavily for a long time. Many say they feel better.

Raising a cow? A little sawdust mixed with its feed will provide bulk. That helps the animal's digestion.

Building a house? Mix sawdust with a special kind of clay and cement to make building blocks or roofing slabs. The mixture is lightweight and easy to use. It also costs less than ordinary concrete.

Like to ice-skate? Toss sawdust onto the surface of a pond as it freezes. The ice will be stronger and safer than normal.

Want to go bowling? Many lightweight balls have cores made of sawdust.

Barbara Gibson

59

Sun power keeps this balloon aloft near Albuquerque, New Mexico. Its inventor, Fredrick Eshoo, keeps the clear-plastic side turned toward the sun. While the sun shines, the balloon has fuel. If clouds block the sun, a small gas tank holds enough fuel for a landing.

60

Sun-powered balloon

Using a gas burner, Fredrick Eshoo of San Francisco, California, inflates his balloon Sunstat. The name combines the word "sun" with part of "aerostat," a term for a lighter-than-air craft.

Fredrick Eshoo had good reason to cheer when he found that his invention really worked. He was in it at the time, soaring high above the ground. Eshoo's invention is a solar-powered balloon.

Hot-air balloons rise when the air inside them is warmer than the air outside. Most depend on gas burners to provide the heat. Eshoo uses a burner to get his balloon off the ground. Then he switches to sun power. One side of the balloon is made of clear plastic. The lining of the other side is black. Sunlight coming through the clear plastic hits the black area and is trapped. This warms the air inside the bag, keeping the balloon aloft.

To land, Eshoo uses battery-operated propellors to turn the clear side of the balloon away from the sun. The air inside cools, and down he comes.

Otis Imboden, NGS (both)

61

You're from where?

Did you ever get a Christmas card from Santa Claus or one from the North Pole? Santa Claus is a town in Indiana, and there is a North Pole in Colorado.

Every Christmas, people send batches of cards to these places to be mailed. They want Santa Claus or North Pole postmarks on the envelopes.

The maps here and on the next pages show some places in the United States that have unusual names. Of course, there are many more.

Odd names often date from pioneer days. Some of the names came from physical features of an area. Others were mistakes in the spelling of Indian or French words. Some towns were named for events that took place there. Some names started as jokes, and they stuck.

One town in New Mexico changed its name, hoping to gain attention and attract visitors and new residents. In 1950, Hot Springs became "Truth or Consequences," the name of a radio show popular at that time. It worked. More visitors came, and the population grew.

Roz Schanzer (62-64)

WASH. · Tumtum · White Swan · Zigzag

OREG. · Looking Glass · Forks of Salmon

CALIF. · Rough and Ready · Fiddletown · Harmony

NEV. · Steamboat · Jackpot · Gold Acres · Plaster City · Needles

IDAHO · Chilly

MONT. · Hungry Horse · Pray · Squirrel

WYO. · Pitchfork · Ten Sleep · Gusher

UTAH · Helper · Bumble Bee · Grasshopper · Cowlic

ARIZ.

COLO. · Dinosaur · North Pole

N. MEX. · Fruitland · Pie Town · Truth or Consequences · Wink

N. · Antelope · Potato Creek · Ig

NE

62

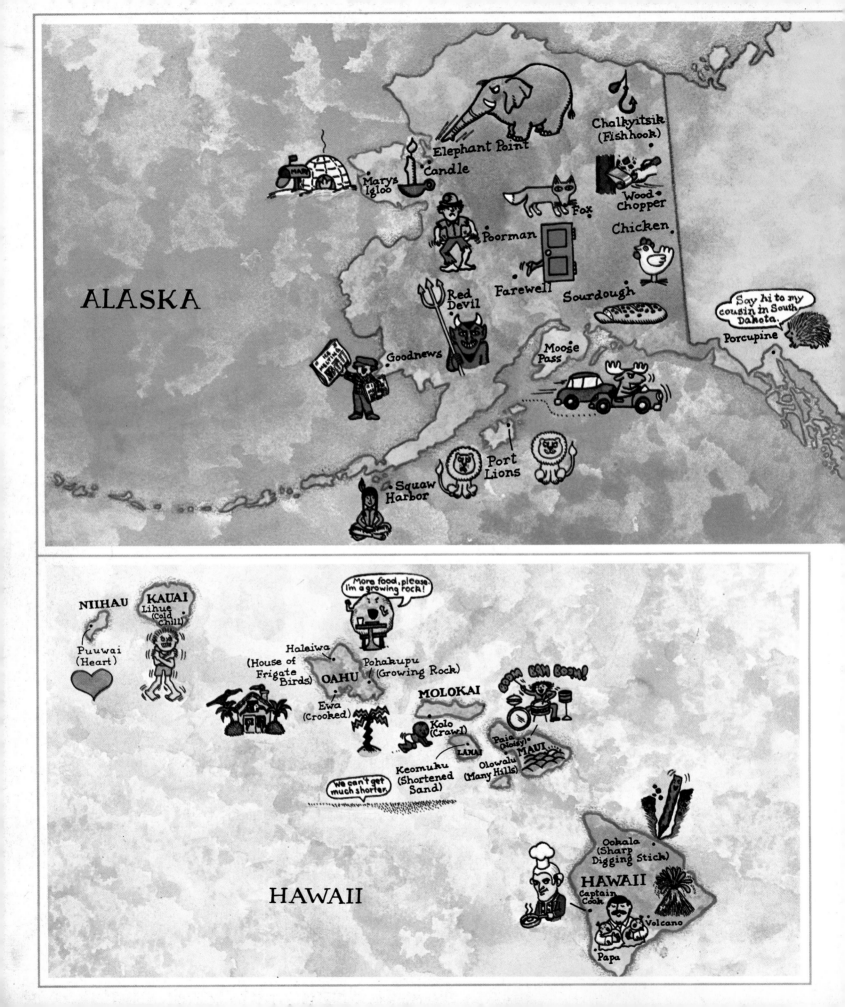

What's it worth?

This huge topaz is the only one of its kind in the world, so no one can say exactly how much it is worth. It can't be priced by comparing it to similar things. But, without doubt, it is worth many thousands of dollars. Its value depends on how much a buyer would be willing to pay if it were offered for sale. The topaz weighs nearly ten pounds (4$\frac{1}{2}$ kg). It is the largest cut gemstone in the world.

Glittering gold

For thousands of years, people have treasured gold. Unlike most other metals, gold has a bright color. It is soft, so it can easily be shaped into jewelry and other ornaments.

Gold doesn't rust or lose its shine. But when silver is exposed to the air, it turns black. Copper turns a dull green. Gold, however, continues to glitter.

There's very little gold in a "gold record." The sale of 500,000 records earns the artist a real record covered with a thin film of gold (below). Gold has come to symbolize excellence. Athletes "go for the gold." When a thing seems perfect, people say it's "as good as gold."

In ancient times, rulers and other important people were often buried with valuable things. The burial mask above was found in an ancient tomb in Greece. The mask is made of pure gold. It probably was buried about 1500 B.C. Nobody knows for certain who wore it. Valued as a clue to the past as well as for its gold content, the mask is a museum piece.

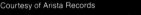

Take a good look at both sides of the gold coin above. There is no other exactly like it. The coin was made in 1907 as a model for $20 United States gold pieces. But President Theodore Roosevelt chose a different design for the new coins. As a result, this coin is now worth a lot more than $20 to collectors. In 1979, it was offered for sale at $895,000!

This bathtub contains $313\frac{1}{2}$ pounds ($142\frac{1}{2}$ kg) of gold. At early 1980 prices, that much gold would be worth between two and four million dollars. Guests at a Japanese hotel pay by the minute for dips in the tub, which is not for sale.

Ancient valuables

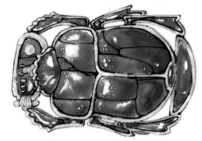

Gemstone from Tutankhamun's tomb
Ancient Egyptians believed blue was the color of the gods. They prized a blue gemstone called lapis lazuli (say LAP-uss-LAZ-uh-lee). Today, people prefer harder gems with more sparkle.

Plants with precious perfume
The frankincense bush and the myrrh tree were two of the most valuable plants in the ancient world. These plants provided fragrant substances. Egyptians and other ancient peoples used them in incense and perfume. The plants grew in southern Arabia. There, chiefs fought to control the routes traders used. Now, most incense and perfume are made from chemicals, not from frankincense or myrrh.

Nothing but the best
Dressed for an important occasion, a royal woman of ancient Egypt (left) wears a gold headdress. It is set with lapis lazuli. She carries incense for the gods and perfumed ointment. Of these riches, only gold has kept its great value.

Lois Sloan (all)

Fancy threads from a sea creature
Only the richest people in the ancient world could wear the soft, gold-colored cloth called sea silk. The raw material came from the pen shell, a mollusk that attaches itself to the seafloor with fine, strong roots. Divers, and fishermen with long tongs, harvested pen shells from the Mediterranean Sea. Spun and woven, the threads made sea silk. Now, machines can make similar cloth cheaply.

Royal purple for the rich
Reddish-purple clothing was a symbol of high status in many ancient lands. It was one of the few dye colors that didn't fade. The dye came from the bodies of Murex snails. Divers brought them up from the seafloor. Now, synthetic dyes in all colors are permanent and inexpensive.

Buggy bone cleaners

HELP WANTED. Bone polishers. Room and board. No salary.

Not many people would answer such an ad. But people aren't wanted. Bugs are.

Scientists at the Museum of Natural History in Washington, D. C., use dermestid (say der-MESS-tid) beetles to help clean bones. After most of the flesh has been removed from bones by humans, the larvae, or young, of the beetles go to work. Larvae have huge appetites. They pick bones bare in a period that may range from hours to months. The cleaned bones are stored for study or for use in exhibits.

It's a soft life! Museum workers keep bones and the larvae of dermestid beetles covered with cotton while the larvae clean the bones. The skeleton of a bird (right) shows evidence of their work.

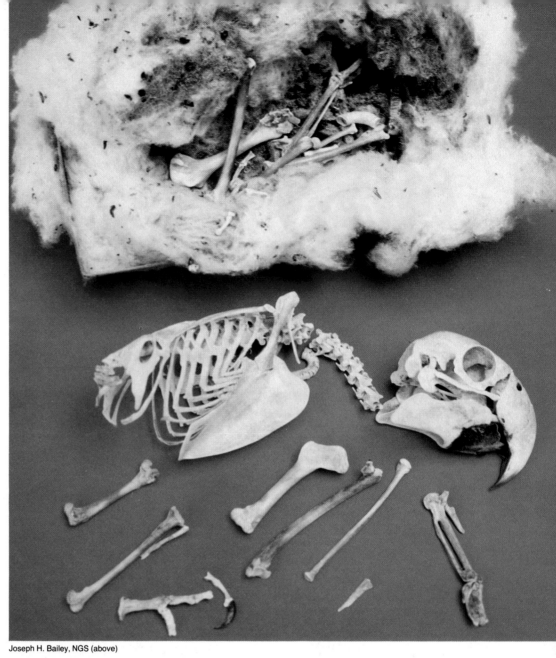

Joseph H. Bailey, NGS (above)

Rick Perry (below)

Fuzzy caterpillar crawls over a bone (above). The caterpillar is the larva of a dermestid beetle. It takes more than a month for a dermestid to change from egg to larva to pupa and, finally, to adult. Careful workers, the larvae can clean even tiny, delicate bones without hurting them.

Who says biggest is best? Not the people who use dermestid beetles as helpers. A tiny adult beetle rests on a fingertip (below). The beetles live in rooms with controlled temperature and moisture. When this beetle was a larva, the food it needed for metamorphosis (say met-uh-MOR-fuh-sis), or change, came from scraps of meat.

68

Eye spies

It seems hard to believe, but people used eyeglasses for about 400 years before someone found a way to keep them planted securely and comfortably on the nose. Italians in the city of Venice invented eyeglasses in the late 1200s. For a long time people had to hold the glasses to their eyes with their hands. Finally, in the 1720s, a London optician made the first eyeglass frames that rested on the nose and ears. At first the earpieces were straight. Soon, people began bending them for a better fit. Before the idea caught on, some curious glasses were in fashion.

In the 1800s, men tried the monocle. Muscles around the eye held a single lens in place. Often the wearer had two lenses, one for reading and one for distance. In time, the monocle gave way to the pince-nez (say pance-NAY). It had a metal spring that connected two lenses. The spring clamped the glasses to the nose. Neither style was very comfortable.

While men wore the monocle, women used the lorgnette (say lorn-YET). It consisted of a pair of spectacles with a hinged handle attached to the frame at one side. When the glasses were not in use, they folded down over the handle.

An early eye aid for reading was the prospect glass, first used in the 1600s. It looked like a toy telescope. Like a telescope, it magnified things. By adding a small side mirror, some people turned the reading glass into a glass for spying around corners.

Jan Watkins

From boulders...

Strange stone faces and other weird shapes greet visitors to Goblin Valley State Park in Utah. Thousands of figures like those shown here fill a large basin surrounded by cliffs.

How did the goblins get into the valley? They were there from the beginning. At first, they were hidden in the thick rock floor of the valley. The floor was made up of both hard and soft rock. Gradually, over many thousands of years, rain wore down much of the softer rock and washed it away. Water trickled into cracks in some rocks and froze. As the freezing water expanded, pieces split off. Finally only parts of the hardest rock and some protected softer rock underneath were left. These became the goblins of Goblin Valley.

What do the stone shapes on these pages remind you of? Employees at Goblin Valley State Park invite visitors to suggest names for the goblins. Those on the right are called "the three gossips." The rock above usually reminds people of a human head. A rock balanced on top looks like a hat.

...to sand

A big boulder that sits around a long time gets weather-beaten. It becomes smaller and smaller. After many thousands of years, it may be part of your sand castle at the beach.

When scientists talk about "sand" they mean very tiny fragments of rock. Each rock size has a different name.

As boulders shrink, they become cobbles, then pebbles, then gravel, then sand. Finally they become bits of silt and dust.

Sand can be used for fun when you're at the beach (right). But sand can also be put to work. Quartz sand is used to make glass, to filter water, and to add a rough finish to sandpaper. Sand is also mixed with cement to make concrete and mortar.

Colorful grains on a greatly enlarged metric ruler (below) are different kinds of sand. Each number marks a centimeter. Sand can be made of many materials. This picture shows, from left: black lava, sea animals and shells, green lava, quartz, gypsum, and rust-colored quartz.

David D. Miller/Tom Stack & Associates

Joseph H. Bailey, NGS

Ridges of sand, called dunes, look like rippling ocean waves (right). Dunes change shape as the wind changes. Steady wind from one direction can make dunes move many feet a year.

David Muench (right)

Stepping out in style

Look at your shoes. What kind are you wearing? Americans buy about a billion pairs of shoes and boots every year. That's more than four pairs for every man, woman, and child.

About a quarter of those shoes are athletic shoes. They are comfortable and last a long time. But many people wear them for another reason: Athletic shoes are stylish. Footwear fads have appeared in every place and time since people began covering their feet for comfort and protection. Both men and women have worn stylish shoes—sometimes with uncomfortable results. So put up your feet, in whatever they're wearing, and read about some odd-looking shoes.

Lois Sloan (all)

Roman emperors wore purple boots decorated with gems, gold thread, and animal skins. Sometimes the animal head was made of gold or ivory.

In ancient Rome, important people wore high boots with open toes. The highest-ranking people wore the highest, fanciest boots. Only the emperor could wear high-topped, richly decorated purple boots like those above. Generals and other important leaders wore shorter, red boots. Members of the senate wore black low-cut models.

In about A.D. 1000, an unusual shoe style for men got a toehold in Europe. Soft leather shoes with pointed toes arrived from Africa and the Middle East. Soon the toes began growing. Men sometimes stiffened them with packing. The tips became so long that people often tripped over them. They had to be fastened to the knees or to the waist. Even with this problem, the style lasted 400 years.

Knights had long toes on their armor to keep their feet in the stirrups.

Stuffed, curled, and sometimes belled, long toes could trip the wearer. The longest were tied to knees or to a belt.

74

When toes came back to earth, they spread out. Fashionable Europeans of the 1500s padded about in floppy shoes. Some were ten inches (25 cm) wide. Stuffing of wool, hair, or hay shaped the soft cloth or leather. The style suited King Henry VIII of England. He had gout, a painful ailment that made his toes swell and ache.

When foot fashion got out of hand, royal decree limited shoe widths to 6 inches (15 cm).

The English called the shoe above a "bear's paw." The one to the left was called a "duck bill."

Wide boots were called bucket tops.

To walk in chopines, women often needed someone to lean on.

Boots had lace trim.

Hip boots began as protection from rough weather. Then 17th-century gentlemen folded them down and added trimming. Gradually, boots grew shorter and fancier. They no longer protected against rain. In fact, the wide tops collected water. But they were handy for carrying scented love notes, gloves, handkerchiefs, and pistols.

For 300 years, stylish women in Europe wore stilt-like shoes. The style came to Italy from the Middle East in about A.D. 1400. At first, shoes with low platforms kept skirts out of the mud. As time passed, the shoes of wealthy women grew higher and fancier. They were called chopines (say shah-PEENS). Some had platforms more than two feet (61 cm) high.

75

Louis XIV of France was only 5 feet 4 inches (163 cm) tall, so he ordered high heels for his shoes. Soon other men were wearing high heels, too. King Louis had his shoes trimmed with lace, ribbons, bows, and jewels. A favorite pair had bows 16 inches (41 cm) across! Not fancy enough, Louis decided. So he ordered famous artists to paint the heels of his shoes with the scenes of battles he had won!

Men in the court of Louis XIV of France wore high-heeled shoes, like the king's. The shoes were trimmed with flowers and bows.

Singing sandals had a bellows in each heel. These worked somewhat like an accordion. As the wearer's heels came up, the bellows filled with air. As the heels came down, they forced air out. Walking produced musical notes.

Ivory flower (left) opened and closed with every step. A spring was hidden in the sandal sole. As the foot came down on the spring, the petals opened. When the foot rose, they closed.

During the 1800s, fashionable Japanese wore unusual sandals. One style had heels that made music. Another had ivory flowers that opened and closed. The woman above balances on slender metal rods at the corners of each shoe.

Africans made shoes from homegrown materials. In the Sudan, lion fur and claws became a boot. In Nigeria, ostrich feathers trimmed a chief's sandals. Designs were sewn on leather boots. The boots had belt loops to hold them up.

Chief wears feather sandals.

Farmers, fishermen, and other workers have clopped around Europe for centuries in heavy wooden shoes. A few people still do. For outdoor work, the shoes have advantages. They keep the feet warm and dry. They last a long time. And they cost very little. In the Netherlands, wooden shoes are called klompen (say KLOMP-en). Instead of hanging up stockings for Santa Claus during the holiday season, Dutch children used to leave a wooden shoe out every night for Sinterklaas and his helper. Now the children use modern shoes.

Wooden shoes once doubled as toys for Dutch youngsters.

Custom-made boots are trimmed with real gems.

People today wear plastic pumps and wooden clogs.

Small mirrors and gold trim an elephant's shoes.

Did you think the shoes on these pages were strange? Then take a good look around you. People still wear wooden-soled clogs, platform shoes, fancy boots, high-heeled shoes, and decorated sandals. They dress up their feet with bows, fur, feathers, and glitter. And they do something that would have seemed really far out 200 years ago. They shape shoes to fit either the left or the right foot.

In India, princes called maharajas (say mah-huh-RAHJ-uhs) rode elephants on special occasions. The elephants sometimes wore fancy shoes.

77

Underwater 'Jim' suit

A new type of diving suit makes its wearer look like an astronaut. And, like an astronaut's spacesuit, the diving suit protects the explorer inside from an environment deadly to human life.

The suit is called "Jim" after a pioneer diver, Jim Jarratt. It is made of very strong metal. The diver inside is safe from crushing water pressure. Air pressure in the suit stays the same as air pressure at sea level.

Jim has its own air supply and temperature control system. A long cord attaches Jim to a support ship. Communication lines keep the diver in touch with people in the ship.

Although Jim looks heavy and clumsy, it gives a diver great freedom of movement. In the water, the suit weighs only about 60 pounds (27 kg). Joints in the arms and legs bend. The diver can walk around on the seafloor.

Four viewing ports let the diver see the underwater world. Jim's arms have hands that look like claws. They can pick things up and hold tools.

The first people to use Jim were divers looking for lost anchor chains. Now, marine scientists are testing Jim to see how they can use it.

Dr. Sylvia A. Earle, a marine

Learning how to move in a new kind of diving gear, Dr. Sylvia A. Earle walks along the floor of the Pacific Ocean. She is 100 feet (30 m) below the surface near Oahu, one of the Hawaiian Islands. A cable and a communications line connect her to a submarine. This dive was a test. Later, Dr. Earle took Jim much deeper.

botanist, took Jim for a walk on the seafloor 1,250 feet (381 m) below the surface. She set a record for the deepest open-sea scientific dive ever made.

You can read more about Jim in the May 1980 issue of NATIONAL GEOGRAPHIC or in the Society's new book, *Exploring the Deep Frontier*.

Jeff Foott, Bruce Coleman Inc.

Marv Poulson

The bristlecone pine is the oldest living thing on earth — and one of the slowest-growing. The tree above took 15 centuries to grow 15 feet (5 m). On high mountain slopes in California, scientists have found many living bristlecone pines more than 4,000 years old! The average pine tree lives no more than 250 years.

Shaped for survival

The boojum (say BOO-jum) is an odd-looking tree. It sometimes grows floppy branches that bend without breaking. The boojum lives on the Mexican peninsula of Baja California, a hot, windy desert. The tree survives in this harsh climate by storing water in a spongy trunk.

This banyan (say BAN-yun) tree is almost a forest by itself. A banyan gets its start in the top of another tree. As birds eat banyan fruit, seeds drop into small pockets of decaying plant matter caught in branches. The seeds sprout and send fast-growing roots to the ground. Each root that takes hold thickens into a tree trunk. Eventually the spreading banyan may kill the host tree.

Derek Fell

Long-lost lotus

The lotus plants shown in this painting came from seeds that may have been more than a thousand years old! Long ago, people in Manchuria, a part of China, grew water plants like these in a lake. When the lake dried up, hardened mud preserved many of the seeds. In the 1920s, a Japanese scientist dug some of them up. He put them in a box. There they remained for 30 years. Finally, in 1951, he gave two of the seeds to an American scientist who took them to Washington, D. C. The seeds were put on damp cotton under a glass cover. They soon sprouted, and grew into lotus plants. Now, their descendants thrive in Washington's Kenilworth Aquatic Gardens. Every summer, thousands of visitors like the boy at right come to the gardens to see these amazing plants.

Lloyd K. Townsend

'Grape tree'

People in some parts of South America pick "grapes" off the bark of trees. A tropical tree called the jaboticaba (say jah-boo-tee-KAH-bah) produces fruit that looks and tastes much like juicy grapes. But the fruit doesn't grow the way grapes do. It develops from fuzzy white flowers that bloom on the bark of the tree. Each flower produces a grape-size fruit. In southeastern Brazil, where many of the trees grow, a town has been named Jaboticabal.

Robert Hynes (both)

Lather up!

Grow your own soap? People in Mexico and the Caribbean islands can. Instead of picking up a box of detergent at the store, people sometimes pick the ripe fruit of the soapberry tree. They slice the berries, toss them into water, and stir. Result: foamy suds that get clothes clean. The shiny brown berries contain a substance called saponin (say SAP-uh-nin). A natural cleaning agent, it works even in cold water from a stream or a lake.

More far-out plants

Fill 'er up—with jungle juice. If you lived in the Amazon rain forest of Brazil and owned trees like these, you might open a diesel-fuel station. Scientists figure that an acre of large Copaifera (say co-pay-IF-uh-ruh) trees can provide as much as 1,050 gallons (3,974 l) of motor fuel a year.

Liquid right from the trees works in diesel motors. The scientists have used it as fuel for their trucks. They say that refining, or purifying, the liquid would make it work even better.

Most people call a cluster of bananas a bunch and think bananas grow with the points down. Not so. A cluster of bananas is called a hand. Each banana is a finger. As the fingers grow, they gradually turn and point upward.

Barbara Gibson (above, top)

Ho, ho! Saved by a jojoba.

Save the whales—with a weed! For centuries, people have hunted sperm whales for their oil. It is used in cosmetics, shampoos, lubricants, and waxes. Now scientists have discovered a desert weed, the jojoba (say ho-HO-buh), that contains the same kind of oil.

Ursula Perrin Vosseler, NGS

Incredible animal

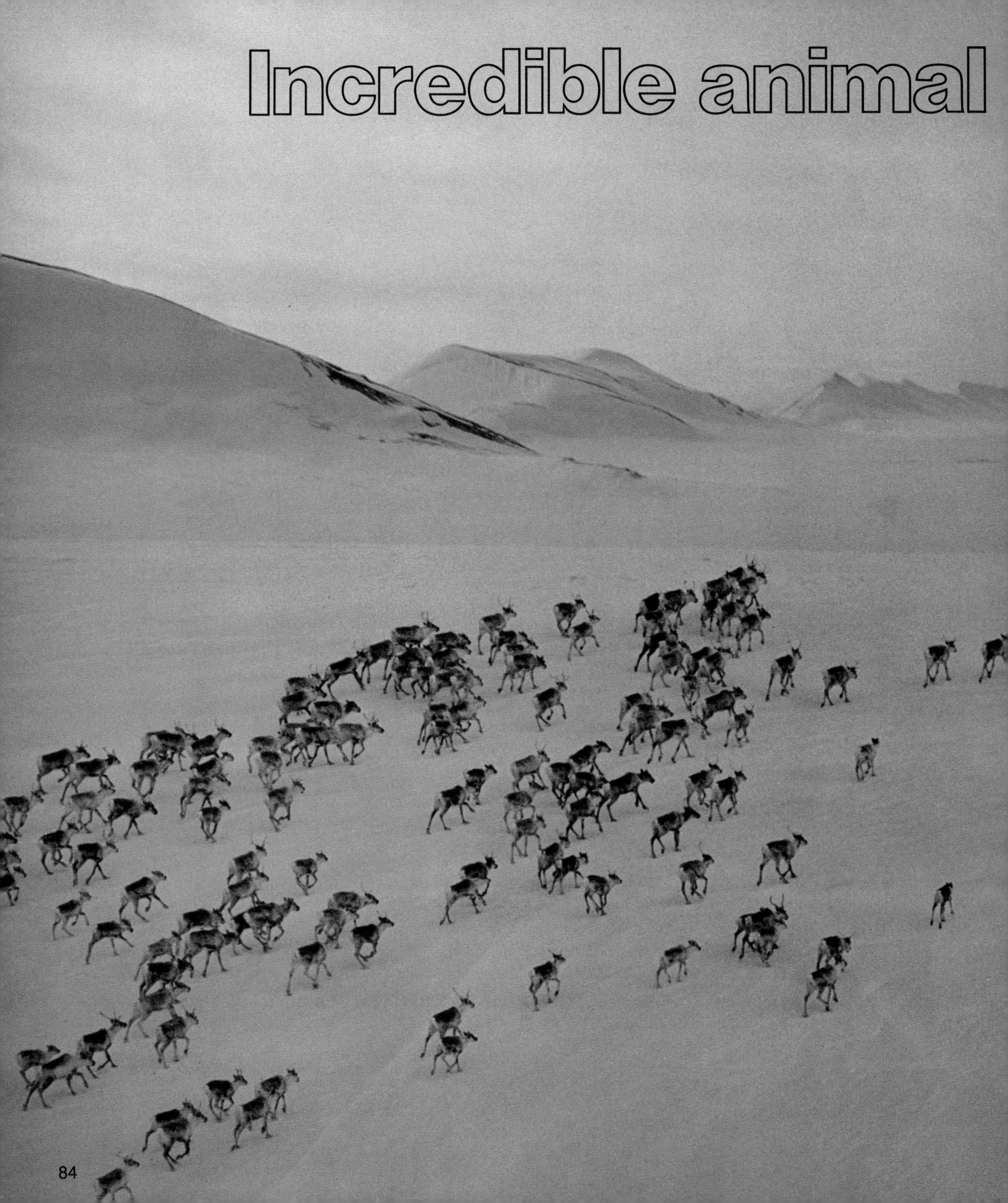

journeys

Facing storms and enemies, some animals make incredible journeys. They migrate long distances to search for food, to escape cold weather, or to lay eggs or raise young where they were raised. On these pages, you'll meet some amazing travelers.

Caribou

Feet clicking as they move, caribou migrate across the northern part of North America and Greenland. Caribou are large deer. Most caribou live in herds. Each spring, they travel to calving grounds, where the young are born. They spend the warm weather in open areas feeding on many kinds of plants. When the first heavy snow falls, they head for wooded ground. There they find small plants called lichens (say LIE-kins) growing on the trees and under the snow.

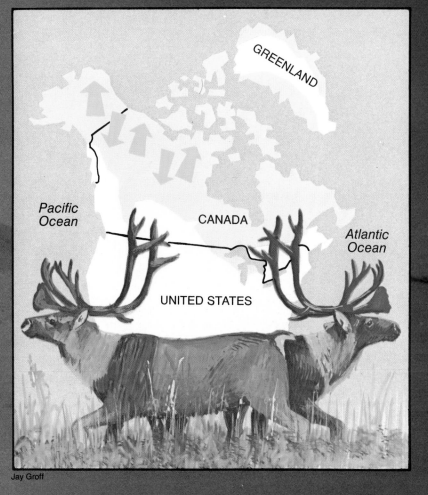

Jay Groff

ENTHEOS

Salmon

Bristol Bay sockeye salmon are hatched in rivers. Most later migrate to the northern Pacific. When they are fully mature, the salmon return to the inland waters where their lives began. There, the adults spawn and die. The eggs hatch, and a new generation starts the cycle again.

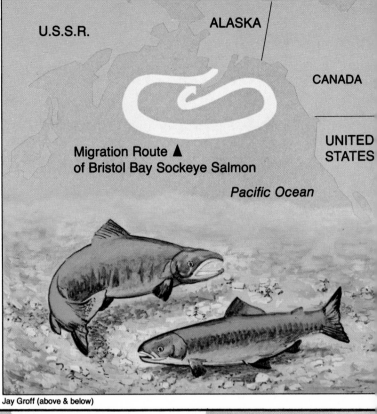

Migration Route ▲
of Bristol Bay Sockeye Salmon

Pacific Ocean

U.S.S.R.

ALASKA

CANADA

UNITED STATES

Jay Groff (above & below)

Jim Brandenburg

Tom Tracy

Geese

Canada geese nest in the north and spend their winters in the south. When it's time to return to the nesting grounds, they make the trip in stages. By following the spring thaw, geese find food and unfrozen water along the way. They fly in V formations. Older birds usually lead, breaking a trail through the air. When one leader becomes tired, it drops back and another bird takes its place. Young geese usually fly in protected positions near the rear of the V.

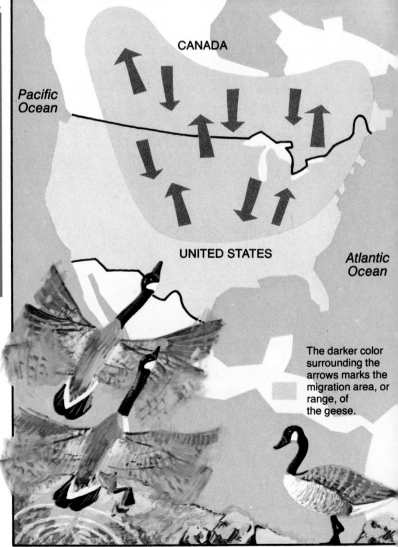

CANADA

Pacific Ocean

UNITED STATES

Atlantic Ocean

The darker color surrounding the arrows marks the migration area, or range, of the geese.

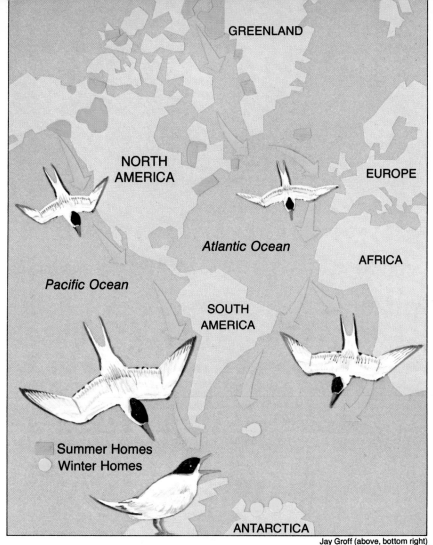

GREENLAND

NORTH AMERICA

EUROPE

Atlantic Ocean

AFRICA

Pacific Ocean

SOUTH AMERICA

▦ Summer Homes
◯ Winter Homes

ANTARCTICA

Jay Groff (above, bottom right)

ENTHEOS

Terns

Imagine having a winter home and a summer home 11,000 miles (17,699 km) apart! Some arctic terns do. Terns nest in the Arctic area. Every autumn, they take off for wintering grounds in Antarctica. By attaching small radio backpacks to some birds, scientists have mapped their routes. Terns hold the long-distance migration record for birds. A tern may live 30 years. In that time, it may travel more than a million miles (1,609,000 km)!

James H. Robinson

Monarchs

Monarch butterflies are small, fragile-looking creatures. But in a single year, some travel 4,000 miles (6,436 km)! Every fall, those hatched east of the Rocky Mountains head for Mexico. Those from west of the Rockies go to California. They spend the winter resting. By keeping quiet, they store fat for the long trip ahead. In the spring, the monarchs fly north, laying eggs along the way. Then they die. The eggs hatch into caterpillars that later become monarchs.

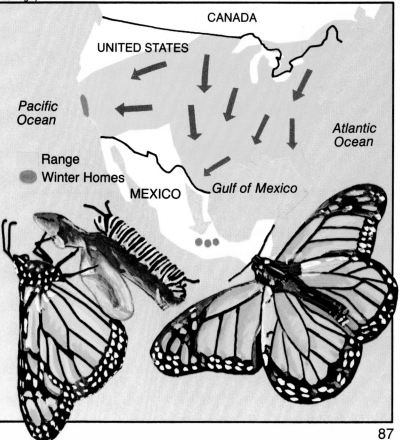

CANADA

UNITED STATES

Pacific Ocean

Atlantic Ocean

Range
◖ Winter Homes

MEXICO

Gulf of Mexico

87

Nick comes home

Selah, Washington

Tucson, Arizona

Dogs don't migrate, but some have returned home over amazing distances. A German shepherd named Nick traveled from Tucson, Arizona, to Selah, Washington!

On a vacation trip, the dog disappeared from a campsite near Tucson. Its owner, Doug Simpson, searched the area for two weeks. Then he gave up hope of finding Nick and left.

Four months later, a thin, dirty German shepherd limped into the Simpsons' yard in Selah. "It's Nick!" Doug's mother shouted. At first, Doug couldn't believe the dog was his. But when Nick nuzzled his hand, Doug was sure!

More than 1,000 miles (1,609 km) separate Tucson and Selah. Doug doesn't know how his pet found the way. But he is glad to have Nick home again!

Paul Salmon

Floating giant

The huge ship in this picture is one of the largest movable objects ever built. Three football fields would fit on its deck, with plenty of room left over. This supersize oil tanker, the *Esso Tokyo,* makes the tug near its stern look like a toy. The giant tanker can carry 120 million gallons (454 million l) of oil in one trip. That's six times as much as the normal-size tanker beside it holds. But the smaller tanker can do some things giants can't. It can go through narrow, shallow channels and into most harbors.

Miles offshore in the Gulf of Mexico, the Esso Tokyo *pumps oil into a smaller tanker. The oil will go to a Texas port. Supertankers cut shipping costs. But most harbors are not deep enough to keep such giants afloat. Some ports have huge buoys in deep water. Supertankers dock there while they unload oil through hoses into underwater pipelines. The pipelines carry the oil to storage tanks on shore.*

Wonderland underground

Hidden away underground is a world few people ever see. It has long tunnels and huge rooms. It has streams and rivers where strange-looking creatures live. It has weird rock formations, and crystals that sparkle like gems. This world is dark, cool, and spooky. It is the world of a cave.

Caves are formed in many ways. Waves may wear away part of a shore. Huge rocks may shift and tilt. Lava from a volcano may harden, leaving air pockets.

Water carves many caves. The water slowly dissolves rock and carries it away.

Caves take many shapes. Some drop straight down, like chimneys. Others form networks of underground tunnels that stretch for miles.

Each cave is a world in itself, an environment that has developed over a long period of time. Living and nonliving things maintain a delicate balance. It can easily be upset. Cavers must use care in exploring this fragile world.

Exploring a pit cave 260 feet (79 m) deep requires special equipment. This caver uses rope-and-harness gear similar to that used by mountain climbers. If you decide to try cave exploring, don't do it alone. Join a group of experienced cavers.

Stepping carefully, a caver crosses a gap in the rocks. It's a 60-foot (18-m) drop to the bottom of this pit! The caver carries a safety rope and wears shoes with non-skid soles. A helmet protects his head from falling rocks. A lamp on the helmet provides light and leaves his hands free.

Climbing back to the surface, a caver pulls himself up on a rope. The caves on these pages are vertical, or pit, caves. All are in the southeastern United States. To see some of the unusual creatures that live in caves, turn the page.

Cave creatures

Deep inside caves, some animals live in total darkness. Many of these animals are blind. How do they survive if they can't see enemies or food? They have organs that are extra sensitive to sound and movement.

Cave creatures usually move slowly. Most of them spend a lot of time at rest. Their habits help them save energy. This means they need less food to stay alive.

Many cave animals have little or no coloring. In the sunlit world, coloring is useful. It protects against burning rays of the sun. It may help an animal attract a mate or hide from enemies. In the dark world deep in a cave, animals don't need coloring.

Not all cave creatures are colorless. Those that live near a cave entrance usually have normal coloring. So do creatures that spend only part of their time in caves, like the bat (right). Bats often use caves as places to rest during the day. At night, they go outside to feed.

Merlin D. Tuttle

John R. MacGregor

◄ Looking for cricket eggs, a cave beetle pokes its feelers into the dirt of a cave floor. The feelers can detect chemicals left by a female cricket when she lays eggs. The beetle eats any cricket eggs it finds.

ANIMALS ANIMALS/Robert W. Mitchell

◄ Feelers alert a cave cricket to disturbances in the air. This helps it find insects to eat. Crickets, in turn, provide food for others. Scorpions hunt them. Beetles eat their eggs. Worms feed on cricket waste.

▲ Although it cannot see, a cave salamander finds prey. Organs in its skin sense slight movements in the water. This salamander has very little coloring, except for its tiny, feathery gills.

◄ Clinging to a rock wall, a little brown bat rests in a cave. Bats can fly in total darkness. They make sounds and catch the echoes that bounce back. From the echoes, they can tell an object's shape, size, and distance. Bats use this ability to find food and to dodge any obstacles in their way.

ANIMALS ANIMALS/Robert W. Mitchell

◄ Like many cave dwellers, this small creature takes whatever food it can find. Feelers guide the isopod (say EYE-so-pod) along the bottoms of pools as it searches for food. It eats all kinds of decaying material from dead leaves to bat waste.

Arlan R. Wiker (both)

▲ Crayfish that live deep inside caves are blind. They are also lighter in color than those found near the surface. They use their long feelers to search for food as they move slowly along the bottoms of streams.

◄ Blind cave fish searches for a meal. Its organs can be seen through its skin. The fish has special sense organs in its skin, as the salamander does. These help it find the smaller water creatures it eats.

Mapping the body

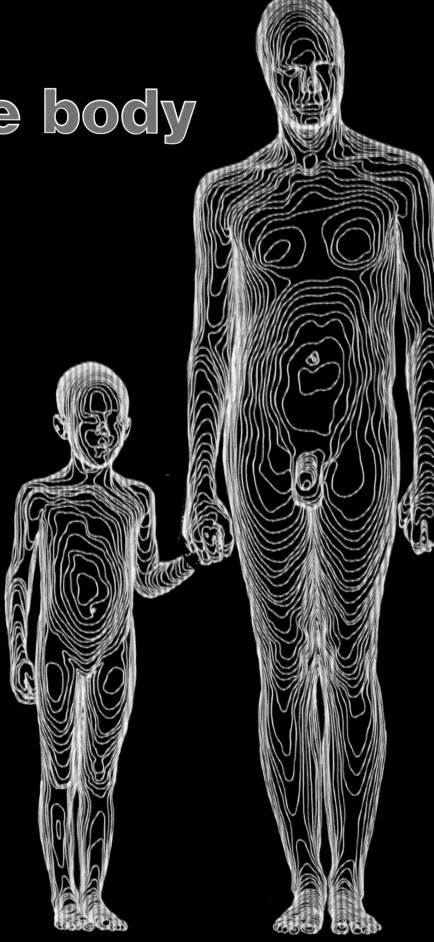

Using special cameras and equipment, scientists make maps of the human body. That's what these pictures are. They show the body as your eyes alone can never see it.

On most of the maps you see, dots mark the towns. Lines represent roads. But some maps, called contour maps, are covered with curved lines. They show the contour, or shape, of the land. With such a map, you can recognize valleys, hilly areas, and steep mountains.

To make a contour map, people first measure the height of the land above sea level. They use lines to show where the height, or elevation, is about the same.

Scientists make contour maps of the human body (right) in much the same way. They use similar techniques to make three-dimensional body maps (far right). "These maps have many uses," says Dan Sheffer, a scientist in Houston, Texas. "We photograph astronauts before they travel into space and after they return. When we compare the photographs, we learn something about the effects of space travel on the human body. The maps help doctors treat patients. Scientists use them to learn more about nutrition and child growth. In the future, we expect to discover even more ways to put body maps to use."

Curving lines form maps of human bodies. Each line represents a measurement. Together, the lines show high and low areas of the body as if they were mountains and valleys on land. Lines close together on feet and heads show steep areas. On flatter areas, the lines are farther apart.

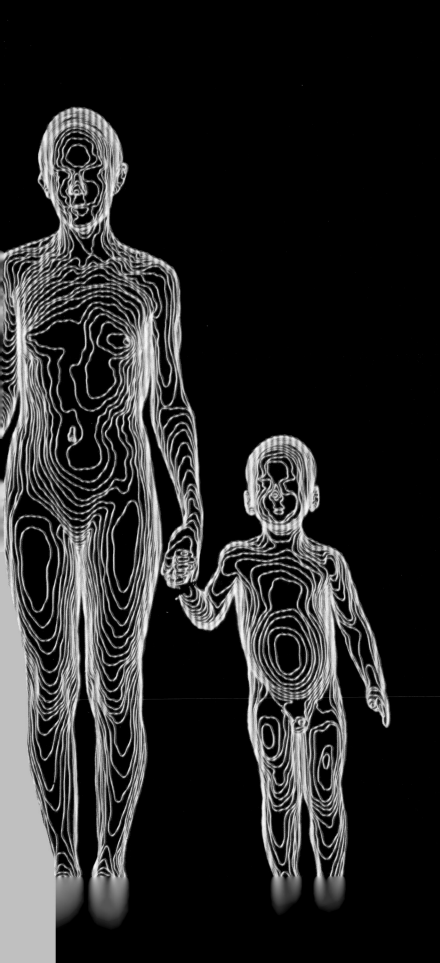

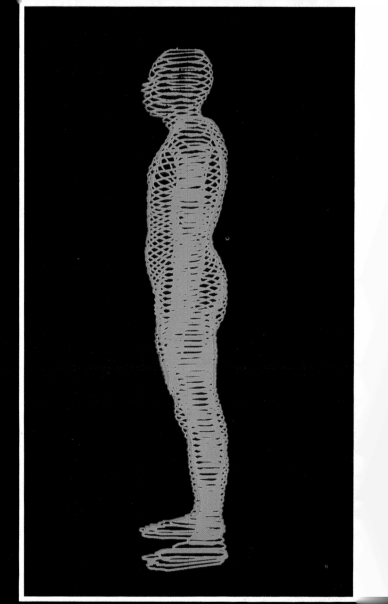

Three-dimensional picture on a computer screen looks somewhat like a wrapped mummy. To make such a picture, cameras photograph a person under flashing lights. The photographs show the body as it looks from the front, back, and sides. At the same time, other equipment takes measurements of the body. When the information is fed into a computer, a picture like this one appears on its screen. Scientists can make the computer turn the image so the body can be seen from any direction. The computer also prints lists of the body measurements. Engineers and scientists use the lists to help them design comfortable airplane cockpits, safer cars, and safety helmets that fit properly.

Cary S. Wolinsky (all)

Gerry Spiess

Small boat, big adventure

All alone, Gerry Spiess sailed his boat, Yankee Girl, *from Virginia Beach, Virginia, to Falmouth, England (left).* Yankee Girl *is so small, ten feet (3 m) long, that the boy in the rowboat easily towed it across the harbor. Spiess built the sailboat at his home in Minnesota. His 3,780-mile (6,083-km) trip took 54 days.* Yankee Girl *survived storms and near collisions to become the smallest sailboat ever to cross the North Atlantic.*

Champion lifter

In one smooth motion, Ann Turbyne hoists 130-pound (59-kg) weights to her shoulders. A pause, a final push, and the weights are above her head. It looks easy, and for Ann it is. These are her practice weights. She can lift much more. "Weight lifting requires some technique," she says. "But it's mostly strength that does the job." Ann, who lives in Winslow, Maine, is the world's champion woman weight lifter. Her best dead lift is 468 pounds (212 kg). Few untrained people can pick up more than 130 pounds.

'Impossible' swim

Watched by crews in nearby boats, Diana Nyad completes a record-setting swim. Diana lives in New York City. She swam 60 miles (97 km) of the Atlantic Ocean from an island in the Bahamas to the east coast of Florida. For 27$\frac{1}{2}$ hours, she battled fatigue, stinging jellyfish, and strong currents from the Gulf Stream that tugged her off course. "Everybody said it couldn't be done," she said as she came ashore — triumphant!

Bruce D. Sutton (bottom)   Mel Dixon (inset)

Crazy contests

Keeping both hands on their brushes, barefoot boys dip deeply into pails of whitewash for the Tom Sawyer Days National Fence Painting Competition. It has been held every July for 24 years in Hannibal, Missouri. Contestants dress as Tom Sawyer, a character made famous by

Americans love to compete, and they love finding new ways of doing it. They stage logrolling contests, hog-calling contests, and contests where people just sit and rock. They race in wacky machines and on homemade rafts. Teams tug ropes through the mud, or push huge balls around fields. Some contests have a serious purpose. But many are held just for fun, or to mark a special event. Here are a few of the not-so-serious ones.

Rick Perry (all)

On your mark. Get set. Crawl! Every summer, a library in McLean, Virginia, has races for creepy crawly things. There are separate events for worms and slugs, caterpillars, and centipedes and millipedes. The first contestant to cross a circle on the sidewalk wins.

98

author Mark Twain, who lived in Hannibal. Boys race to a section of fence and cover it with whitewash. They try to paint neatly, and fast. Most finish in about seven seconds.

Everyone sees red at a relay race in Cedar Springs, Michigan, a place known for the red flannel underwear made there. One team member runs to a pile of flannels, untangles a set, and jumps in. The racer dashes to a partner and passes on the flannels. The partner then races for the finish line, as Jeff Hall, 14, is doing here.

Eating ice cream can be tough. Debbie Bartholf and Ahlke Heydemann, both 16, tried for the Guinness record at a contest in Gaithersburg, Maryland. Twenty entered, but no one broke the existing record: 3 pounds, 6 ounces (1½ kg) in a minute and a half.

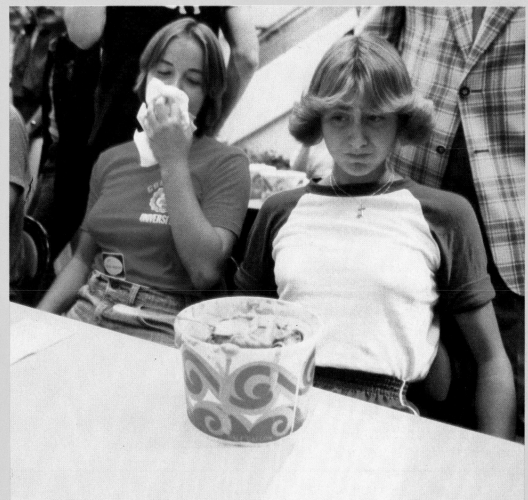

A-mazing mouse

Flip a switch and this mouse will explore, figure out, and memorize the fastest way through a maze. The photograph below, a double exposure, shows the inner workings of the amazing ten-inch (25-cm) robot. The mouse, named Moonlight Special, competed against 16 other robots in the first Amazing Micro-Mouse Maze Contest. It was held in New York City in 1979. Micro-mouse contestants had three chances to run the maze. On the first two tries, they "learned" the pattern. A few made the third run without mistakes. Prizes were given for speed and for learning ability.

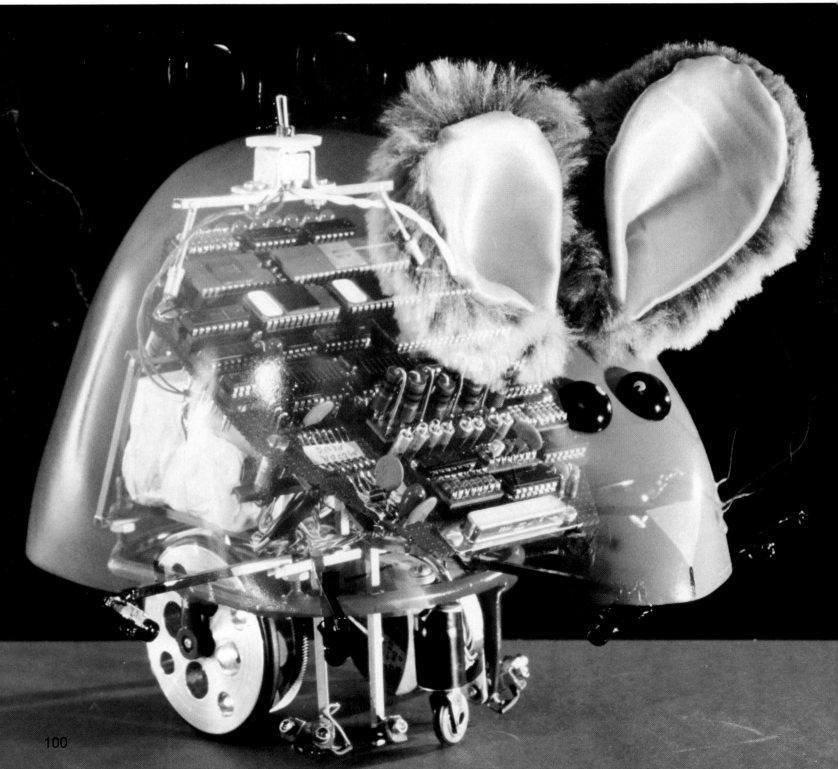

...and now you know

There is a North Pole in the United States (page 62).

There is very little gold in a "gold record" (page 66).

You'd wear out long before the pencil would if you set out to draw a continuous straight line with one (page 20).

Sawdust can be used to improve a lot of things — from cattle feed to ice (page 59).

A certain kind of beetle has a boiling-hot surprise in store for its enemies (page 58).

The *Gossamer Albatross* made an amazing 22-mile (35-km) flight: Human leg muscles, not an engine, powered the plane across the English Channel (pages 14-16).

Photographers use special techniques to create far-out pictures (pages 46-49).

A train conductor of 100 years ago inspired the inventor of the electric computer (page 33).

There's a place in the United States where it rains more than it does anywhere else in the world (page 25).

Meat-eating plants attract — and trap — insect prey (pages 34-39).

In the age of Louis XIV, high-heeled shoes with fancy trimmings were all the rage for men (page 76).

Cave-dwelling creatures manage to hunt food and avoid enemies — even though many are blind (pages 92-93).

You'd have to live more than 4,000 years to match the age of the oldest living things on earth (page 80).

There's a job perfectly suited to the person who doesn't want to move a muscle (pages 8-9).

You can pay by the minute to bathe in a gold tub (page 66).

A lizard snares insects with a tongue that can stretch longer than its body (pages 52-53).

A woman weight lifter practices by hoisting 130 pounds (59 kg) over her head and has set a women's record of 468 pounds (212 kg) (pages 96-97).

An arctic tern may fly a million miles (1,609,000 km) or more in its lifetime (page 87).

COVER: *Jeffrey Cowan, 16, of Washington, D. C., is a professional magician, so he is used to pulling odd things out of a hat. Here, his magic hat yields a high-jumping dolphin, a soaring balloon, a space-walking astronaut, and a flipped-over gymnast.*

BOOK COVER:

Joseph Lavenburg, NGS (magician)

James A. McDivitt, NASA (astronaut)

O. Louis Mazzatenta, NGS (balloon)

Joseph H. Bailey, NGS (gymnast)

Lowell Georgia (dolphin)

BALANCING ACT:
Leaning over, standing on one foot, or upside down like this gymnast, people can keep their balance. Fluid in the inner ear helps. Every time you change position, the fluid moves. Hair-like cells in the ear sense this movement and send messages to the brain. The brain signals the muscles. They adjust and keep you balanced — most of the time.

Index

Bold type refers to illustrations; regular type refers to text.

CONSULTANTS

Dr. Glenn O. Blough, *Educational Consultant*
Dr. Nicholas J. Long, *Consulting Psychologist*

The Special Publications and School Services Division is grateful to the individuals, organizations, and agencies named or quoted in the text and to the individuals cited here for their generous assistance:

Walter Berry, Rust Engineering Company
Eriik Blom, Smithsonian Institution
Dr. Thomas E. Bowman, Smithsonian Institution
Dr. Ray Cameron, Alaska Department of Fish and Game
John Campbell, Texas Instruments
Dr. Lanny Cornell, D.V.M., San Diego Sea World
Dr. Ralph E. Crabill, Smithsonian Institution
Ronald I. Crombie, Smithsonian Institution
Paul Desautels, Smithsonian Institution
Loren Dunton, Kwatro Corporation
Marvin D. Erickson, Battelle, Pacific Northwest Laboratories
Dr. C. W. Ferguson, University of Arizona, Tucson
Dr. Douglas Ferguson, United States Department of Agriculture
Lorraine Forestiere, Forestiere Underground Gardens
Irene de B. Galvin, United States Department of Agriculture
Virginia Garvey, The Banana Bunch
A. Les Gaver, National Aeronautics and Space Administration
Dr. Valerius Geist, University of Calgary
Jerry Goldberg, Real-Rich Ice Cream
Dr. Betty L. Hamilton, Georgetown University School of Medicine
Dr. Charles O. Handley, Jr., Smithsonian Institution
Dr. Lindesay Harkness, Harvard University
Gary Hevel, Smithsonian Institution
Dr. Horton H. Hobbs, Jr., Smithsonian Institution
Dr. John R. Holsinger, Old Dominion University
James H. Horan, Finfair
V. Glenn Horstman, Battelle, Pacific Northwest Laboratories
Epel Ilom, Micronesia Washington Office
Phyllis Ingram, Dolley Madison Branch, Fairfax County Public Library

Professor Nandini Iyer, University of California at Santa Barbara
Werner Janney
Douglas John, Smithsonian Institution
Jay Jorden, National Speleological Society
Dr. Bela Julesz, Bell Telephone Laboratories
Robert H. Kanazawa, Smithsonian Institution
Dr. Jean Langenheim, University of California at Santa Cruz
Mike Lozon, Cedar Springs Clipper
William N. Lyons
Dr. Paul MacCready, Aerovironment, Inc.
Dr. Raymond B. Manning, Smithsonian Institution
Larry E. Matthews, National Speleological Society
Bryce Montgomery, Utah Division of Water Resources
Dr. David A. Nickle, Smithsonian Institution
Dr. Paul A. Opler, Office of Endangered Species, United States Fish and Wildlife Service
Etziko Penner, Japan National Tourist Office
Shepard Perrin, Louisiana Superport Authority
Dr. Joseph Rosewater, Smithsonian Institution
Mark Roth, Smithsonian Institution
Carol Salsman, Tony Lama Boot Company
Dr. Dan Sheffer, The Institute for Rehabilitation and Research
Dr. Roy Sieber, University of Indiana
Leo Song, California State University at Fullerton
Bruce Stephens, San Diego Sea World
Stephen J. Traiman, Recording Industry Association
Dr. Fred A. Urquhart, Scarborough College, University of Toronto
Dr. Gus W. Van Beek, Smithsonian Institution
Dr. J. Kim Vandiver, Massachusetts Institute of Technology
Dr. Maurice H. Vaughan, University of Pittsburgh
Dr. Noel D. Vietmeyer, National Academy of Sciences
Jan Wampler, Architect
Horace V. Wester, National Park Service
Terry White, National Aeronautics and Space Administration
Dr. Don E. Wilson, National Fish and Wildlife Laboratory, United States Fish and Wildlife Service
Dr. George Robert Zug, Smithsonian Institution
Max Zupon, Kennecott Minerals Company

Library of Congress CIP Data

Far-out facts.

(Books for world explorers)
Includes index.

SUMMARY: Unusual facts about a wide range of topics including plants and animals, earth sciences, manners and customs, photography, and history. A poster-size calendar, and a 24-page booklet of games and puzzles are included.

1. Science—Miscellanea—Juvenile literature. [1. Science—Miscellanea]
I. National Geographic Society, Washington, D. C. II. Series.
Q163.F228   031'.02   79-1793
ISBN 0-87044-319-4
ISBN 0-87044-324-0 (lib. bdg.)

PUBLISHED BY
THE NATIONAL GEOGRAPHIC SOCIETY
WASHINGTON, D. C.

Robert E. Doyle, *President*
Melvin M. Payne, *Chairman of the Board*
Gilbert M. Grosvenor, *Editor*
Melville Bell Grosvenor, *Editor Emeritus*

PREPARED BY THE SPECIAL PUBLICATIONS
AND SCHOOL SERVICES DIVISION

Robert L. Breeden, *Director*
Donald J. Crump, *Associate Director*
Philip B. Silcott, *Assistant Director*

STAFF FOR BOOKS FOR WORLD EXPLORERS SERIES: Ralph Gray, *Editor;* Pat Robbins, *Managing Editor;* Ursula Perrin Vosseler, *Art Director*

STAFF FOR FAR-OUT FACTS: Pat Robbins, *Managing Editor;* Thomas B. Powell III, *Picture Editor;* Drayton Hawkins, *Designer;* Alison Wilbur, *Assistant Picture Editor;* Ross Bankson, Alice Berman, Jan Leslie Cook, James A. Cox, Gayle Cramer, Elaine S. Furlow, Roger B. Hirschland, Rochelle Moskowitz, Anne H. Oman, Maureen Palmedo, Edith Pendleton, Ania Savage, Karen Skeirik, Gene S. Stuart, Sharon W. Walsh, *Writers;* Jennifer West Lodge, Tee Loftin, *Researchers;* Carol A. Enquist, Alice K. Jablonsky, Bonnie S. Lawrence, Marilyn L. Wilbur, Peggy Winston, *Assistant Researchers*

ILLUSTRATIONS AND DESIGN: Beth Molloy, Louise Ponsford, Lynette Ruschak, *Design Assistants;* John D. Garst, Jr., Peter J. Balch, Lisa Biganzoli, Mark H. Seidler, *Geographic Art*

FAR-OUT FUN!: Patricia N. Holland, *Project Editor;* Ross Bankson, Mary B. Campbell, Roger B. Hirschland, Karen Skeirik, Gene S. Stuart, *Writers;* Jennifer West Lodge, Tee Loftin, *Researchers*

ENGRAVING, PRINTING, AND PRODUCT MANUFACTURE: Robert W. Messer, *Manager;* George V. White, *Production Manager;* Raja D. Murshed, June L. Graham, Christine A. Roberts, Richard A. McClure, *Assistant Production Managers;* David V. Showers, *Production Assistant;* Susan M. Oehler, *Production Staff Assistant*

STAFF ASSISTANTS: Debra A. Antonini, Pamela A. Black, Barbara Bricks, Jane H. Buxton, Kay Dascalakis, Mary Elizabeth Davis, Rosamund Garner, Nancy J. Harvey, Jane M. Holloway, Ellen Joan Hurst, Suzanne J. Jacobson, Artemis S. Lampathakis, Cleo Petroff, Marcia Robinson, Katheryn M. Slocum

INTERNS: Ruth Amy, Mary B. Campbell, Liza Carter, Rebecca Anne Garrett, Betsy L. Grasso, Nancy Herlihy, Glover Johns III, Jennifer Johnston, Mary Clare Kenning, Abby Dana Livingston, Amy E. Metcalfe, Janet C. Poort, Frances Anne Root, Kayna Kemp Stout, Margaret J. Tinsley, Leslie E. Tompkins, Cobie van L. Maas, Phyllis C. Watt

MARKET RESEARCH: Joe Fowler, Patrick Fowler, Karen A. Geiger, Carrla M. Holmes, Cynthia B. Lew, Meg McElligott, Stephen F. Moss

INDEX: Sarah K. Werkheiser

Composition for FAR-OUT FACTS by National Geographic's Photographic Services, Carl M. Shrader, Chief; Lawrence F. Ludwig, Assistant Chief. Printed and bound by Holladay-Tyler Printing Corp., Rockville, Md. Color separations by the Lanman Companies, Washington, D. C.; Progressive Color Corp., Rockville, Md.; The J. Wm. Reed Co., Alexandria, Va. *Classroom Activities Folder*, produced by Mazor Corporation, Dayton, Ohio.